ANDREW MONTGOMERY

ITN
50

YEARS OF NEWS

E-S-P

ITN 50

The first 50 years

First published in Great Britain in 2005 by ESP Publishing
17 Fenlock Court, Blenheim Office Park, Long Hanborough, Oxon,
OX29 8LN. Tel. Telephone: 01993 882027 Email: sales@e-s-p.eu.com

Copyright © ESP Publishing 2005

Text copyright © Andrew Montgomery 2005

Photographs copyright © ITN Archive 2005 Unless Specified

Jacket & page 200 Twin Towers Photograph © Corbis,
Page 10 Berlin Wall Photograph © Corbis, Page 32 Mini Photograph ©
Corbis, Page 74 Concorde in Flight Photograph © Corbis, Page 118
Iranian Embassy Seige Photograph © Corbis, Page 158 Saddam
Hussein & Sons Uday and Qusay Photograph © Corbis.

1 3 5 7 9 8 6 4 2

British Library Cataloguing-in-Publication Data: A catalogue record for
this book is available from the British Library

ISBN 0-9550356-0-0

Edited by Marie Wilson
Designed by HL Studios Ltd
Printed and bound in Spain

Contents

For half a century ITN cameras have covered the world, capturing the events and changes which have shaped our lives since those first black-and-white ITN images flickered onto television screens in 1955. The pages of this book recall the highlights of that 50-year-span in the same way they were delivered by ITN into the homes of millions of viewers day by day.

ITN started out with a mission to report the news differently. "News is human and alive and we intend to present it in that manner," declared ITN's first editor, Aidan Crawley. ITN has stuck to that philosophy ever since – always striving to find the human dimension in its news coverage, making news accessible, relevant and immediate. ITN has also looked for the offbeat and humorous to lighten the serious business at the heart of the news agenda.

The pictures in the book are taken from original ITN film and show world events just as they appeared on our television screens over the 1955-2005 period – which is how most of us remember them. The history of ITN itself is intertwined with the spirit of each changing decade and with the lives of many hundreds of members of staff – past and present. There are anchors and reporters in this book who became household names and won the affection of millions, but there are many whose work behind the scenes made years of brilliant news reporting. There are those who committed their working lives to producing the most vivid and compelling news coverage, those who showed immense courage in getting the story and those who tragically gave their lives in pursuit of their chosen calling.

ITN has always been a company rich in energy, imagination and innovation. The spirit which infused ITN at the start still burns brightly in the ITN of today. ITN's news services for ITV and Channel 4 have become even more renowned in the recent past for their exclusives and for their stunning coverage of events ranging from the Tsunami disaster through to the London bombings, and to the New Orleans floods.

The sprit of enterprise and dynamism is also very much alive and visible in the ITN of today. ITN is now in the forefront of the evolving new media markets, managing the world's largest database of video footage and leading the field in delivery of new video services to mobile phone platforms and broadband.

ITN built a name as one of the world's great news organisations in its first 50 years. It remains at the top of its game in news and is now building a name as a pioneer in shaping the media markets of tomorrow. ITN's next half century promises to be every bit as exciting as the last one.

This book is a tribute to all who built the ITN name. In the process they revolutionised the way news is presented and changed the way news organisations treat the people who ultimately matter – the viewers at home.

Mark Wood

ITV News Team

Nicholas Owen

Nicholas Owen is the co-presenter of the ITV *Lunchtime News* – alongside Katie Derham. His first taste of reporting was for the *Surrey Mirror* in 1964. He worked subsequently for the *Evening Standard* in London and *The Daily Telegraph* and was with the *Financial Times* for seven years. In 1981 he joined the BBC in Newcastle, working on *Look North*, but also covering general and industrial stories for national BBC news and current affairs programmes. He moved to ITN in 1984 as the Business and Economics correspondent of *Channel 4 News*. During the 1991 Gulf War he presented the highly acclaimed *Midnight Special* programmes on Channel Four and he was also one of the original presenters of *The Parliament Programme*, also on Channel Four. From 1994 to 2000 Nicholas was Royal Correspondent for *ITV News*. During that time he covered the break up of the marriage of the Prince and Princess of Wales. He also reported on the Princess's death and its aftermath and commentated during ITV's coverage of her funeral. He has published a book on her life, entitled *Diana the People's Princess*.

Mary Nightingale

Mary Nightingale is the co-presenter of the ITV Evening News, the news service produced by ITN for ITV. Mary joined ITV News team in January 2001 and has presented across a range of ITV News programming.

In March 2002 Mary won the prestigious Newscaster of the Year award from the Television & Radio Industries Club (TRIC). Until April 1999 Mary was co-presenter with Alastair Stewart of London News Network's flagship news programme London Tonight and was the sole presenter of London Today, Carlton's lunchtime magazine programme. She has also presented the daily late news bulletins of London Tonight. Mary started her journalism career as a presenter and writer on World Business Satellite for TV Tokyo, going on to work for BBC World Service Television's World Business Report. Mary also worked for Reuters Financial Television in 1994 and, in 1995, presented weekend editions of ITN's World News.

Andrea Catherwood
Presenter

James Mates
Senior correspondent

Nina Hossain
Presenter

Channel 4 News Team

Alex Thomson

Alex Thomson is presenter and Chief Correspondent for ITN's Channel 4 News. Alex has covered 23 wars and many other major conflicts around the world during his 17 years with ITN.

He won the 1997 Home News Award at the Royal Television Society Journalism Awards for his investigative reports surrounding the events of Bloody Sunday. His coverage of the BNP by-election victory in Millwall won the same award in 1993 and his work in Bosnia contributed to Channel 4 News's BAFTA- winning coverage from 1995. During 1990 Alex covered the 'velvet revolution' in Czechoslovakia and his reports won the RTS award for best International News coverage that year.

Alex joined C4 News in 1988 as a reporter. Before that Alex reported for the BBC in Belfast. He is also a published non-fiction author having written about India and media censorship during the 1991 Gulf war.

Alex lives in Essex with his partner, investigative TV reporter Sarah Spiller. They have twin sons.

Samira Ahmed
Presenter

Gary Gibbon
Political Editor

Sarah Smith
Anchor More4News

Krishnan Guru-Murthy

Krishnan Guru-Murthy is the anchor of Channel 4 News at Noon and is one of the regular presenters of the flagship Channel 4 News evening programme. Krishnan joined the team as a presenter and reporter in 1998 when the programme expanded into broadcasting seven days a week. Since joining Channel 4 News he has covered a variety of events at home and abroad including earthquakes in India and Turkey, the conflict in Kashmir, the Potters Bar train crash and American politics. During the Iraq War he fronted Channel 4's coverage during the day, presenting the Channel 4 Morning News and the lunchtime War Report. Before joining the Channel 4 news team in June 1998 Krishnan presented BBC News 24's 1200-1600 strand since the launch of the service in November 1997. From 1994 until his move to News 24, Krishnan worked mainly as a reporter on BBC2's 'Newsnight' and presented the weekend news on BBC World. He was also part of the live broadcast team for the funeral of Diana, Princess of Wales in 1997.

Lindsey Hilsum
International Editor

1950s

You've never had it so good...

Harold Macmillan

After the misery of the war years, dark, depressing and austere, the country stood on the brink of a brighter future in the 1950s. By 1957, the Prime Minister, Harold Macmillan was able to sum it up in that famous phrase – 'You've never had it so good'. Industrial production and wages were rising. There were plenty of things to celebrate too; the Festival of Britain, the conquest of Everest and the Queen's Coronation. You no longer needed to go to the cinema to see it all happen. The new medium of television gave people a ringside seat in their own home. ITN News, on the new commercial channel ITV, revolutionised the way we watched history in the making.

For a nerve jangling, exhilarating month they'd been rehearsing and preparing dummy programmes. News crews had raced to locations to film material that would never be seen. Interviews had been conducted that would never be heard. Newscasters had been practising, standing behind a picture frame to read their scripts to get the idea of appearing on a television screen – cameras weren't operational until a day before transmission. Engineers had wrestled with bulky, temperamental equipment in the new television studio at Television House in Kingsway in the centre of London.

Then, at 10pm on September 22nd 1955 the 'On Air' lights glowed for the first time in that studio. ITN's first programme – and first newscaster Christopher Chataway – appeared on screen; but only to viewers in London and the home counties, which was the limit of ITV's reach on that first night. It began with a title sequence that showed cans of ITN film being rushed to Television House, underscored by a suitably urgent signature tune entitled 'Non-Stop'. A look in ITN's hand-written diary of the first bulletin reveals the 'running order' of reports: *Policeman Interview outside Guildhall – 14 secs'*. It was at an elaborate ceremony, at Guildhall in the heart of the capital, that ITV had been launched; the policeman talked about the crowds outside. After that, *'Macmillan at Foreign Press Lunch – 64 secs'* was the Foreign Secretary and future Prime Minister insisting nuclear weapons ensured world peace. He called it his *'There ain't gonna be no war,'* theory. Then a *'Lost session at the United Nations'*, the marriage of *(Austrian) Princess Ira von Fürstenberg'*, at the age of 15, and *'the Rocky Marciano / Archie Moore weigh-in'*. And on it went, hurricane in the USA, Italian fashions, motorcycle scrambling, water skiing. On Day One, ITN had managed to include most of the essential ingredients that make up the desired daily diet of the British news viewer: politics, crime, royalty, romance combined with human interest. It had completed its first broadcast as scheduled and has continued do so for half a century. Apart from Christmas Day that year. As the Library diary records: *'25th December. No transmissions. Hurray!'*

Above: Lynne Reid Banks, ITN's first female reporter, during an interview with film maker Darryl Zanuck in February 1957.

Above: During his visit to England in 1955, Evangelist Billy Graham talked to ITN about changes in scientific education in the US.

Above: Like all celebrities before and since, American singer Eartha Kitt agreed to be interviewed to publicise her forthcoming personal appearances.

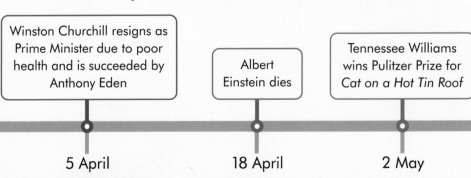

Start of guerrilla campaign against British government in Cyprus

Winston Churchill resigns as Prime Minister due to poor health and is succeeded by Anthony Eden

Albert Einstein dies

Tennessee Williams wins Pulitzer Prize for *Cat on a Hot Tin Roof*

1 April   5 April   18 April   2 May

The original team – numbering around 150 people – was overseen by the first editor of ITN, Aidan Crawley. He'd only been given the job of starting ITV's news service six months earlier. It was he who introduced the concept of newscasters, rather than newsreaders. They became the faces of ITN programmes – familiar and trusted – rather than the somewhat anonymous BBC announcers who read the news scripts. In addition to Christopher Chataway, there was Robin Day – later of *Panorama* and *Question Time* fame – who read the 7pm bulletin. Barbara Mandell – who Crawley made Britain's first woman newscaster – read the bulletin at lunchtime.

A former Daily Mail journalist, Aidan Crawley was an accomplished documentary maker, and had been a member of Parliament. During the war he'd been a fighter pilot so he was used to command structures and discipline; qualities that stood him in good stead.

Among the items that appeared in those first, hectic weeks, were interviews with the entertainer Eartha Kitt and the evangelist Billy Graham, who was in Britain for some of his crusades. There was even an appearance by the philosopher and humanitarian Albert Schweitzer.

Disneyland had opened in California earlier in the year but, as ever, there was no shortage of bad news to report. James Dean died in a car crash, South Vietnam declared itself a Republic, South Africa withdrew from the United Nations and a State of Emergency was declared in Cyprus.

Above: Billy Graham packed Wembley Stadium with enraptured crowds ready to embrace the Word, when he appeared there in November 1955.

Above: Dr Albert Schweitzer poses for ITN cameras outside Cambridge University, where he is to be awarded an honorary degree in October 1955.

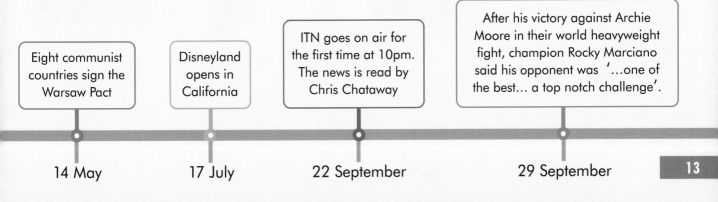

Eight communist countries sign the Warsaw Pact

Disneyland opens in California

ITN goes on air for the first time at 10pm. The news is read by Chris Chataway

After his victory against Archie Moore in their world heavyweight fight, champion Rocky Marciano said his opponent was '...one of the best... a top notch challenge'.

14 May

17 July

22 September

29 September

Above: Foreign secretary Harold Macmillan speaks at a lunch with foreign press. He told them: 'We are approaching a point when no power, however great, can hope to win a war. In nuclear war, once this saturation point is reached, there can be no victor. There can only be mutual and universal destruction...'

War time leader Sir Winston Churchill announced he was stepping down as Prime Minister. He was 80. The grand old man of British politics told reporters he accepted he couldn't carry on in the job any longer. He was succeeded by Sir Anthony Eden and having agreed the timing of the handover, Sir Winston said 'No two men will ever change guard more smoothly'. But Churchill stayed on as an MP – and fought and won his parliamentary seat when Eden called an election just two weeks after taking over. Eden's Conservative party won with an increased majority.

In Cyprus there were violent demonstrations against British rule. A state of emergency was declared after British troops were killed in terrorist attacks. Cypriot police, backed by British troops, were stoned by gangs of youths when they tried to break up illegal processions and demonstrations.

A story closer to home attracted the attention of ITN news editor, Arthur Clifford. A Labour MP, Norman Dodds, had published a newspaper article claiming that, since the end of the war, the British workman had grown lazy. This was based on observations that Dodds had made of a group of road menders working outside his office. He had taken time, presumably from his Parliamentary and Constituency business, to record how many hours the men actually spent working as opposed to drinking tea and smoking Woodbines. Dodds's article caused considerable upset and provoked much debate. Clifford, in a truly inspired move, somehow managed to persuade him to join the very workmen whom he had spied on, in their hut, over mugs of tea, to thrash out the matter. It made wonderful television and ITN had proved it could make news out of human interest stories.

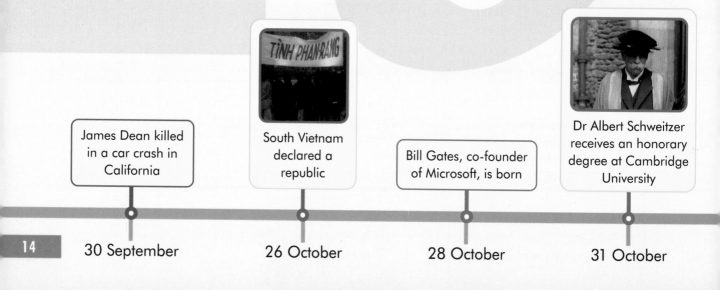

James Dean killed in a car crash in California

South Vietnam declared a republic

Bill Gates, co-founder of Microsoft, is born

Dr Albert Schweitzer receives an honorary degree at Cambridge University

30 September   26 October   28 October   31 October

Sir Christopher Chataway

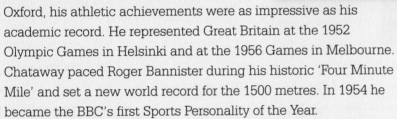

Christopher Chataway was born on January 31st, 1931. Educated at Sherborne School and Magdalen College, Oxford, his athletic achievements were as impressive as his academic record. He represented Great Britain at the 1952 Olympic Games in Helsinki and at the 1956 Games in Melbourne. Chataway paced Roger Bannister during his historic 'Four Minute Mile' and set a new world record for the 1500 metres. In 1954 he became the BBC's first Sports Personality of the Year.

His first job was with Guinness, the well-known Dublin brewers and it was during his brief tenure there that he put forward his Oxford contemporaries, Ross and Norris McWhirter, as joint editors of the newly proposed *Book of Records*.

He joined the embryonic ITN and read the first news broadcast on September 22nd 1955. The following year he joined the BBC but was already becoming directly involved in politics. In 1958 he was elected to the London County Council and subsequently became Conservative MP for Lewisham North. Having held ministerial rank, he retired from politics in 1974, at the age of 43, and began yet another successful career in business. He became chairman of the Civil Aviation Authority and was also instrumental in creating the London Marathon. He was knighted in 1995.

Above: Fifteen-year-old Austrian Princess Virginia (Ira) Furstenberg just after her wedding to 31-year-old Prince Alfonso Maximilian Hohenlohe Langenburg.

Above: The wedding was in Venice, so the bride and groom left the church by gondola.

The Cocos Islands are transferred from United Kingdom to Australian control

Clement Attlee resigns as leader of the Labour Party – his successor is Hugh Gaitskill

23 November

7 December

The Suez crisis was the major story of the year and it provided ITN – and newcaster Robin Day – with the chance to change television news interviews for ever. His direct style of questioning Egypt's President Nasser had never been seen before on British television. Until then, the standard interview question more or less amounted to: 'Is there anything else you'd like to tell us, Mr President?' Day cemented ITN's challenging approach and his reputation as the country's leading political interviewer for a generation. Now, for the first time, viewers at home could see an international leader being asked to explain himself – in President Nasser's case, about his views on Israel's right to exist.

Above: Salvage ships in operation in the Suez Canal, clearing the blockage of ships.

The crisis had begun in June. British troops had policed the canal zone for nearly 70 years but under a new treaty signed in 1954, that responsibility passed to the Egyptians.

Less than a fortnight after the handover, Colonel Gamal Abd al-Nasser, as he was then, was elected President. In July, enraged by the reluctance of Britain and the United States to help in financing the construction of the Aswan High Dam, Nasser nationalised the canal. The Americans made an unsuccessful attempt to arrange a deal under which the canal could be controlled by the Suez Canal Users' Association. The British, under Prime Minister Anthony Eden, then entered into secret negotiations with the French – originally co-owners of the canal with them – and the Israelis. Their idea was that Israel would launch an invasion of Egypt and advance towards the canal zone. The British and French would then issue an already

Above: The Royal West Kents marching to their craft with their kitbags, as they prepare to leave Suez at the end of the crisis.

Release of Elvis' single 'Heartbreak Hotel', which goes to No.1 in the US pop charts

Grace Kelly marries Prince Rainier

First explosion of a hydrogen bomb on Bikini Atoll in the Pacific Ocean

January

19 April

21 May

agreed ultimatum to Israel to withdraw, whereupon an Anglo-French force would be sent in to 'protect' the canal. It was a distinctly risky plan, but the exclusion of the United States from its planning and preparation was nothing short of suicidal.

The result was a fiasco. Israeli armour advanced into Sinai; British and French artillery bombarded the canal zone; paratroopers were dropped; bombs were dropped; and, crucially, US support for sterling was dropped. Russia came to Egypt's aid, turning the Cold War yet colder, and a rift was opened between the Western Allies: President Eisenhower was furious at what looked to all the world to be the heavy-handed imperialism of the British and the French. Eden, mentally and physically shattered by the affair, was forced to resign at the start of the following year.

As with Suez, ITN captured and held the attention of the public during the uprising in Hungary. Martin Gray, a cameraman who had gained experience during the Second World War, managed to slip across the border from Austria on a daily basis. He'd drive 200 miles to Budapest and film for a couple of hours, before returning to Vienna to ship his film back to London. After a few hours sleep, he'd do the same thing all over again. He managed to keep it up for several days and obtained some dramatic footage of Stalin's statue being toppled, Russian tanks burning in the streets and the terrible vengeance being wrought on the hated secret police. The United Nations was distracted by the Suez Crisis and failed to react to the desperate pleas broadcast by Budapest's *Freedom Radio*. Martin Gray's pictures then gave viewers the story with the arrival of Soviet tanks in Budapest to crush the Hungarian revolution. Thanks to him, ITN viewers saw it happen.

Above: Hungarian refugees with their children; they fled the city on foot with just a few possessions as Soviet tanks advanced on Budapest.

Above: The Suez crisis caused a serious shortage of petrol in Britain, and petrol stations soon sold out and had to close.

Marilyn Monroe marries Arthur Miller

Marilyn arrives in London to start filming *The Prince and the Showgirl* with Sir Laurence Olivier

Elvis appears on the Ed Sullivan Show

Donald Campbell achieves a new water speed record

29 June

14 July

9 September

20 September

Above: American film star Grace Kelly stands at the altar of Monte Carlo cathedral, waiting for her prince.

Above: Bill Haley, with his trademark kiss curl in evidence, interviewed during a visit to Britain.

Right: Prince Rainier and the new Princess Grace of Monaco during the course of their wedding by Monsignor Marella. The bride's parents had front row seats at the social event of the year.

The celebrity culture of the modern media is nothing new. Back in 1956, royalty – the real and the movie variety – was a key component of ITN's news bulletins. In a notable wedding the two combined in what seemed like a fairy-tale – Prince Rainier of Monaco married the actress Grace Kelly. She'd visited Monaco two years previously, during the shooting of Alfred Hitchcock's *To Catch a Thief*, but only met her handsome prince at the film's launch in Cannes. They became engaged within a fortnight and their wedding, attended by over 1,200 guests, was the most glamorous event to be covered since the coronation of Queen Elizabeth II. It was watched by a worldwide television audience of over 30 million people – a huge number for the time. Before her wedding Grace Kelly was contractually obliged to complete her last movie for MGM. It was appropriately *High Society*.

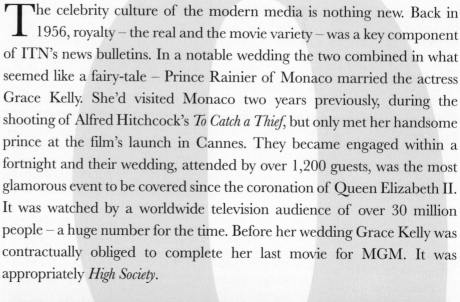

Uprising in Hungary against communist government

Suez crisis

Eisenhower re-elected

Summer Olympic Games begin in Melbourne, Australia

23 October

October/November

6 November

22 November

Far left: Sixteen young couples competing in a rock 'n roll dance contest. The loud music and fast moves demanded stamina as well as dancing skill.

Left: One of the young dancers throws his partner high into the air. Older people disapproved of young girls showing their underwear as they danced.

Above: A Teddy boy was judged by the flamboyance of his quiff – which hairdressers could extend by adding a 'sausage' of false hair in the centre.

That other screen legend, Marilyn Monroe, was at the height of her fame. She had split up with Joe DiMaggio, married Arthur Miller, and formed her own production company. She came to London with her new husband to make *The Prince and the Showgirl*, co-starring Laurence Olivier, at Pinewood studios. ITN news editor Arthur Clifford dispatched Robin Day to the Savoy Hotel to interview Marilyn. In a gesture of chivalry, Day took the rose from his buttonhole and presented it to the star, who wasn't quite sure what she was supposed to do with it. But it made good television.

A new form of celebrity was emerging in the mid-fifties – the rock 'n roll star. To the disapproval of parents everywhere, rock 'n roll arrived in Britain from the United States. 'Rock Around the Clock', by Bill Haley and the Comets, was one of the biggest hits in history and was quickly taken up by teenagers everywhere, keen to find their own kind of music, as different from their parents' as possible. Elvis had also appeared on the scene, with his unique mixture of rock and country and western that became known as Rockabilly. But Britain was soon to come up with its own rock bands and much of what made this style of music unique – its ability to unite audiences and adapt new influences – came from them. Coupled with disapproval of the music, older people often also disapproved of teenagers' style of dress, as Teddy Boys came into fashion with their quiffed hair, drainpipe trousers and dressy coats.

Above: Victor Mature and Marilyn Monroe waiting to meet Queen Elizabeth II at a Royal Film Performance of *The Battle of the River Plate* in London.

Suez crisis causes petrol rationing in Britain

Castro lands in Cuba

Japan is admitted to the UN

23 November

2 December

12 December

Above: Harold Macmillan makes a speech to the nation after becoming Prime Minister, paying tribute to Anthony Eden and talking of the task ahead.

After Anthony Eden's resignation over the Suez crisis, Harold Macmillan succeeded him as Prime Minister in January. There had been petrol shortages as a result of Suez but the mood of the country was improving. By the middle of the year, Macmillan was telling the public: 'You will see a state of prosperity such as we have never had in my lifetime – nor indeed in the history of this country. Indeed, let us be frank about it, most of our people have never had it so good'.

A young Prince Charles was, it seemed, enjoying his school days at Hill House in West London. ITN cameras filmed him at sports day watched by his parents. The Prince introduced them to his friends and then got down to the serious business of playing cricket and taking part in sprint and relay races. But six months after arriving there, the eight year old Charles was on the move, to Cheam Preparatory School near Newbury. Once again, ITN cameras were there as his trunk, bearing the label 'HRH Prince Charles' was carried in. He was to stay there for the next five years. Changing schools would not have been newsworthy, but for the fact that Prince Charles was the first heir to the throne to attend school. His mother, like others before her, had been educated by governesses or teachers at home.

In Monaco, Prince Rainier and Princess Grace celebrated the birth of their first child, Caroline. When she was old enough to go to school her parents solved the problem of whether to send her away or educate her at home in a novel and imaginative manner: they built a school within the royal palace and invited local children to attend.

Harold Macmillan becomes Prime Minister after Sir Anthony Eden resigns

10 January

Cavern Club opens in Liverpool

16 January

Ku Klux Klan members force truck driver to jump off bridge and drown

23 January

Film producer Darryl Zanuck is interviewed by Lynne Reid Banks for ITN

23 February

Lynne Reid Banks

Lynne Reid Banks was born in London in 1929. She was evacuated to Canada during the war, following a brief period in a Convent School. On her return to London in 1945 she began work in repertory theatre and then took up writing as a freelance journalist and playwright. Her play *It Never Rains* was broadcast by the BBC on Easter Sunday 1954 and the following year she became Britain's first female TV news reporter, working for ITN. In 1960 her proto-feminist novel The *L-Shaped Room* was published, to considerable critical acclaim. She left ITN two years later, the book having already been made into a film, to emigrate to Israel.

She lived on a kibbutz, working as a teacher, for the best part of a decade. During this time she met and married Chaim Stephenson, a sculptor, and they had three sons. In 1974, Lynne returned, with her family, to London. She and her husband moved to Dorset in 1985.

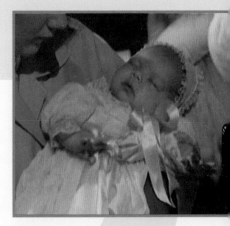

Above: The new baby Princess Caroline sleeps through all the fuss at her christening.

Above: Princess Grace, holding Princess Caroline, and Prince Rainier appear on the balcony of the palace in Monaco.

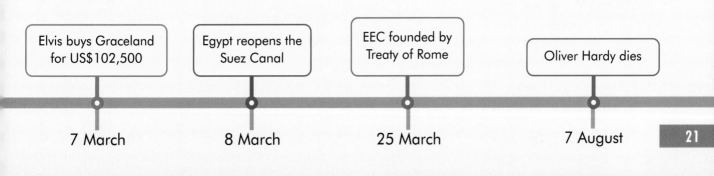

Elvis buys Graceland for US$102,500	Egypt reopens the Suez Canal	EEC founded by Treaty of Rome	Oliver Hardy dies
7 March	8 March	25 March	7 August

1957 Science

Above: An animated representation of *Sputnik II*, on its way into space after sections one and two had broken away.

ITN covered the launch of the Soviet *Sputnik I* satellite with one of its half hour *Roving Report* programmes, which had begun that year. The launch itself, in October, had surprised the world. It was, in effect, the start of the space race and the Soviets didn't stop there. Next they sent a dog called Laika, which means 'barker', into space on board *Sputnik II* in November.

The giant radio telescope at Joddrell Bank in Cheshire came into service and was able to track these events. Sadly, there was no method of retrieving *Sputnik II* and so Laika died in space. ITN reported the protests by animal lovers outside the Soviet Embassy in London.

The Soviets had seized the upper hand in the space race that, over the next decade, was to be closely tracked by ITN.

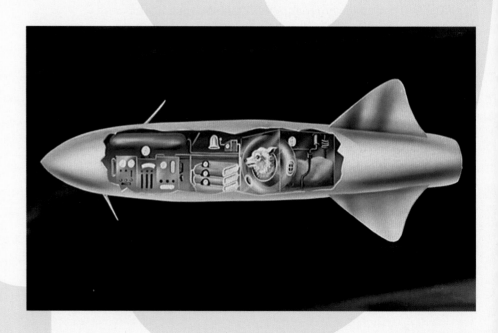

Right: A cutaway diagram of *Sputnik II* showed details of the equipment and Laika, a husky dog. The Soviets had asked the British for help in tracking the spacecraft, using the giant radio telescope at Joddrell Bank.

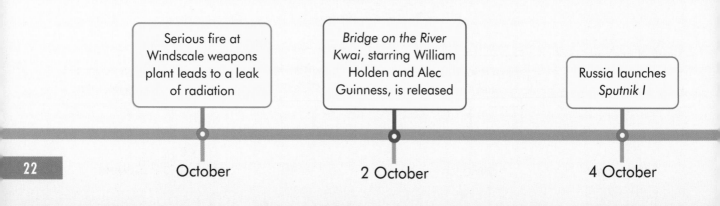

Serious fire at Windscale weapons plant leads to a leak of radiation

Bridge on the River Kwai, starring William Holden and Alec Guinness, is released

Russia launches *Sputnik I*

October

2 October

4 October

ITN faced the sensitive task of reporting findings by the British Medical Association that there was a link between smoking and lung cancer. In those days there were cigarette adverts on ITV – lots of them. When ITN was established, there had been warnings about possible conflicts of interest in the reporting of stories that involved advertisers. But ITN did report the story, believing it was important news and believing advertisers wanted unbiased news programmes around which they could place their commercials. There had been a lot of interest in the issue due to the death, in 1952, of George VI from lung cancer. And of course the vast majority of Britain's adult population, male and female, were habitual smokers.

Above: Actor John Mills, with his daughter and wife, arrives at a film premiere. The film industry was appealing for lower taxes, and to stop the closure of small local cinemas.

Above: Hopalong Cassidy (aka Bill Boyd) appears at Battersea Fun Fair, throwing 'hopalong' coins to excited children.

Above: A young boy catches one of Hopalong's coins, and gleefully displays it to the camera.

Above: Calypso singer Lord Kitchener in London, where he composed and sang a song to celebrate the independence of Ghana.

Joddrell Bank radio telescope starts operating in Cheshire

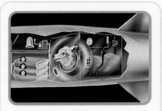

Russia puts a dog, 'Laika', into space in *Sputnik II*

First televised Queen's Christmas Speech

11 October

3 November

25 December

Above left: The Manchester United team pose for cameras as they board their plane in Manchester, at the start of the ill-fated trip.

Above middle: The wreckage of the BEA airliner at the airport in Munich. 23 people lost their lives, including players Duncan Edwards, Mark Jones, Eddie Colman, David Pegg, Tommy Taylor, Roger Byrne, Geoff Bent, Liam Whelan and Team Secretary Walter Crickner.

Above right: Rescue workers toiled amidst the wreckage in case anyone was still left alive. Some survivors of the crash had gone back into the flames to try and rescue others.

February 6th 1958, is a date that will be forever remembered by football fans around the world. A tragic, heartbreaking accident resulted in almost a whole team of young players being killed. They were, of course, the Busby Babes of Manchester United – then, as now, one of the most famous and popular football clubs in the world. Manager Matt Busby and his young team had won the respect and affection of the nation with their electrifying performances both at home and on the continent. In 1957, Manchester United became the first British team to be invited to compete in the European Cup Championship and reached the semi-finals. They were defeated by the eventual winners, Real Madrid. In the same year they made it to the FA Cup Final but were beaten by Aston Villa. They did, however, win the League and so qualified once more for the European Cup Competition in 1958.

In the quarter finals that year, United travelled to Belgrade and back, via Munich. A 47-seat, British European Airways aircraft had been chartered to take the team, along with their officials, newspaper reporters and even a few fans. The Belgrade pitch had to be cleared of snow before the match could begin. By half time, Manchester United were 3–0 ahead but, at the end, it

Aircraft crash at Munich kills eight Manchester United players

Pope Pius XII declares Saint Clare to be the patron saint of television

The last debutantes go to Buckingham Palace to be presented

Elvis is inducted into the US army

6 February   17 February   18 March   24 March

was a three-all draw. That was fine, as the team were through to the semi-finals, and they boarded the return flight in high spirits. The weather at Munich, where they had to land for refuelling, was fiercely cold and icy and there was slush on the runway. Two takeoff attempts had to be aborted; on the third, the pilots lost control of the aircraft and it careered off the end of the runway, crashed into a house and caught fire. Despite this, some of the survivors went back into the plane to try to rescue others. The final death toll was 23. ITN didn't receive pictures of the wreckage, with police searching through it, until the following morning. They showed the front section of wrecked fuselage, as heavy snow fell in the darkness. Two days after the crash two survivors, who were both *Daily Mail* journalists, returned to Heathrow airport, where they were interviewed by Reggie Bosanquet. One described how everybody just longed to get home and wanted to get on the plane, despite the treacherous weather. The other described sitting by the window watching the wheels churning up snow. Then he realised they were no longer on the runway and as the plane pitched, he braced, ready for impact.

Four days after the crash ITN cameras were allowed into the hospital to film some of the surviving team members. Matt Busby was in an oxygen tent. He survived. So did Bobby Charlton, Ray Wood and Jackie Blanchflower. Duncan Edwards, who was also filmed that day, did not.

Above left: In Manchester, news-stand placards proclaim the grim news.

Above middle: Manager Matt Busby was critically injured, and at first there were fears that he would not survive. The other badly-injured players who survived were Bill Foulkes, Ray Wood, Dennis Violett and John Berry.

Above right: As news of the tragedy broke, the flag at Old Trafford, Manchester United's home ground, flew at half-mast.

Above: In May, a demonstration marching on a government building in Algiers turned into a riot as stones were thrown. The Algerian National Liberation Front had been trying to oust their French rulers since 1952.

Khruschev becomes Premier of the Soviet Union	First passenger jet service is launched by BOAC	*Gigi*, starring Leslie Caron and Louis Jourdan, is released
27 March	2 May	15 May

Hula hoops had the world in a spin in 1958. They started off in the United States but as the film archive reveals, they were popular in Britain, France, Germany, Poland, Japan and Korea. 20 million were bought within the first six months of the hula hoop going on sale – queues outside shops selling the hoops were filmed around the world. They had become such a phenomenon that even the British Medical Association felt the need to issue a health warning about them. They described the twisting involved as 'very energetic exercise, and great caution is necessary. No one with a known heart disease should try it, and anyone who is out of training but otherwise fit should not go hard at it right away. Muscles should be loosened up for a week or two at first'. Some people suggested promoting hula hooping as a weight loss exercise. One 12-year-old British girl entered a fairground contest and managed to keep going for seven hours and five minutes before she collapsed. She was successfully revived with a drop of brandy.

Below left: According to a news report from Germany, the craze for hula hoops had reached such a level that this girl even took hers to the dentist!

Below right: The craze was popular with young girls. It was surprisingly difficult to keep the hoop spinning round your waist unless you were particularly fit and supple.

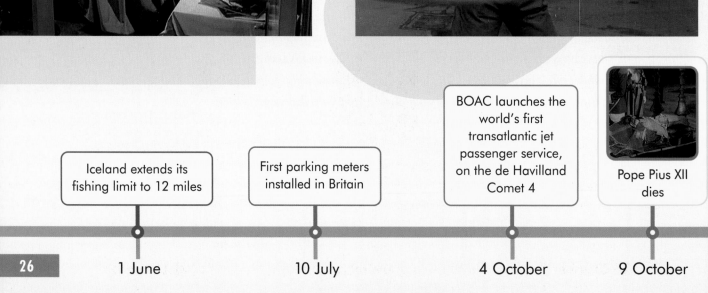

Iceland extends its fishing limit to 12 miles

First parking meters installed in Britain

BOAC launches the world's first transatlantic jet passenger service, on the de Havilland Comet 4

Pope Pius XII dies

1 June

10 July

4 October

9 October

Elsewhere in the world, Elvis Presley joined the United States army; Soviet leader Nikita Kruschev visited China's Chairman Mao; Charles de Gaulle was re-elected President of France; Pope Pius XII died and Iceland extended its fishing limit to 12 miles. Dark clouds gathered over Aden, Malta and Algeria – and British Overseas Airways Corporation (BOAC) introduced the world's first transatlantic jet service using de Havilland Comet 4s.

Above: Elvis Presley at a press conference, after being inducted into the US army to do his national service. After training, he was posted to Germany.

Above: Charles de Gaulle addresses the French National Assembly, after having accepted the offer to form a National Government.

Above: The funeral of Pope Pius XII in Rome – he was succeeded by Pope John XXIII.

Boeing 707 flies a passenger service across the Atlantic

Pope John XXIII is crowned

Charles de Gaulle elected President of France

26 October

6 November

21 December

ITN tackled its first general election programme – without two of its biggest stars. Both Robin Day and Ludovic Kennedy had decided to stand as parliamentary candidates for the Liberal Party. Replacing them wasn't ITN's only challenge as the new ITV network wasn't used to coming together for a big occasion like election night. But ITN did pioneer one aspect of election coverage that year, which is still going strong today – the swingometer. As the night progressed, the swingometer showed Macmillan had increased his majority at the expense of the Labour Party. He said later, 'this election has shown that the class war is obsolete'.

In the same election, a young woman called Margaret Thatcher became Honourable Member for Finchley.

At the end of August, America's President Eisenhower flew to London for talks with Macmillan and to cement the special relationship between the two countries. As he arrived at Heathrow airport, the President, who was stationed in Britain during the Second World War, said he was pleased to be back in the land that he'd come to love and to see some of his warmest friends. The following day ITN cameras were in Balmoral for the President's visit to see the Queen. Two nights later ITN unveiled part of a new type of broadcast to the nation. It showed Macmillan and Eisenhower in what became known as their fireside chat. They were filmed in Downing Street, sitting opposite one another and talking in a relaxed way, less stuffy and formal than the normal political broadcasts. Eisenhower talked about the possibility of a summit with the Soviet leader, Nikita Khrushchev, the following year. Macmillan thanked Eisenhower for coming to Britain and drew things to a close, saying they had to go and meet guests, including Winston Churchill. And with that, they got up and walked off into an adjoining room.

After the Munich air crash of the previous year came another. Buddy Holly and two of his band members were killed when a chartered light aircraft crashed near Mason City in Iowa. He, his band and his roadies had drawn lots to see who would fly home in the plane and who would travel in the unheated tour bus. All the passengers and the pilot were killed when the four seater plane crashed soon after taking off in a blinding snowstorm.

Below: Prime Minister Harold Macmillan meets US President Eisenhower, who was visiting Britain in August 1959. Ike had been based in Britain during the Second World War, and was held in high regard by the British people.

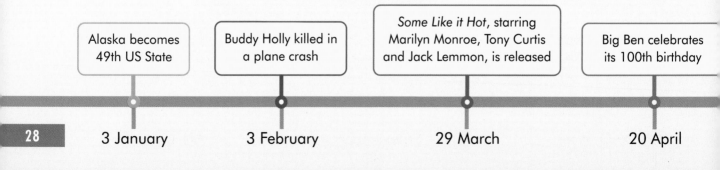

| Alaska becomes 49th US State | Buddy Holly killed in a plane crash | *Some Like it Hot*, starring Marilyn Monroe, Tony Curtis and Jack Lemmon, is released | Big Ben celebrates its 100th birthday |

3 January   3 February   29 March   20 April

Sir Robin Day

'I shudder to watch interviewers who think it clever to be snide, supercilious, or downright offensive'.

Son of a telephone manager, Robin Day was born on October 24th, 1923, in Gloucester, where he attended Cripps School. He was subsequently sent to Bembridge School on the Isle of Wight until 1940, when the school was moved to Coniston in the Lake District. He served in the Royal Artillery from 1943 to 1947 and then went up to St Edmund Hall, Oxford, to read Law. He became President of the Oxford Union in 1950, leading a debating team on a tour of the United States. He was called to the Bar in 1952 but after only one year in practice took up the post of Press Officer to the British Information Service in Washington. He joined BBC Radio in 1955 but immediately applied for a post as newscaster with ITN, just as it was starting up. In 1956 Day pulled off a memorable and dramatic coup by securing a filmed interview with President Nasser in the wake of the Suez crisis.

He ran for Parliament as Liberal candidate for Hereford in 1959 but failed to be elected. He returned to television – back at the BBC – gaining respect and admiration as a political commentator and interviewer. He chaired *Question Time* for a decade and his trademark bow tie and gruff delivery endeared him to a wide audience. He received his knighthood in 1981. He died on August 7th, 2000, from heart disease. He wrote two autobiographies: *Day by Day* (1975) and *The Grand Inquisitor* (1989).

Above: Engineers study a wooden model of the new VC10 jet passenger plane, being developed by Vickers Vanguard in Weybridge, Surrey.

Above: In Bedfordshire, inventor Emiel Hartman was working on another flying machine – the ornithopter. Pedal-powered, the contraption had feathered wings that flapped like a bird's.

Queen Elizabeth II opens the St Lawrence Seaway

Jack Brabham wins the Driver's World Championship Grand Prix

Singapore becomes a self-governing Crown Colony

25 April

14 May

3 June

Above: The 1959 Ideal Home Exhibition, as usual, showed all the latest equipment for the home. By this time the annual exhibition was an integral part of popular culture.

ITN covered the *Daily Mail* Ideal Home Exhibition at Olympia for the first time in 1959. Viewers saw Europe's first fully-automatic washing machine in action. These annual exhibitions, of all things home-related, had proved to be immensely popular since the first one held, amazingly, way back in 1908.

Nylon was the must-have fabric of the age and a Nylon Fair was held in London to demonstrate the clothes that could be made from it. There was imitation seal skin, fake beaver and mink, women's nightwear and lingerie, and even several displays of bridal gowns. Norman Hartnell, the designer of the Queen's coronation dress six years earlier, displayed a nylon bridal outfit, complete with beads and sequins. The first nylon carpets were on display too – mothproof, of course.

Right: At the Nylon Fair in London the latest fashions were revealed for the first time – with everything made in nylon, even these orange leggings and floaty housecoat.

Far right: Nylon stockings were a great invention – although it was not too long before they were replaced with tights.

Fortieth anniversary of the first transatlantic flight

Cliff Richard releases 'Living Doll'

Hovercraft SR N1 crosses the Channel

18 June

10 July

30 July

Nylon had been invented by Wallace Carothers, an American chemist, working for the DuPont Company, in Wilmington, Delaware, in 1935. The popular tale of the name being derived from the fact that it was developed in two laboratories, one based in New York and one in London isn't true. There was no British involvement at all and DuPont considered around 400 different names. One possible explanation is that nylon is a corruption of 'no-run'. Carothers himself wanted to call it Fibre 66. However the name came about, the fabric was very popular and when Barbie made her debut in 1959, her first set of clothes was made out of nylon.

Above: A unique view of Britain's first motorway, the M1 – no traffic! It opened for the first time in November 1959.

Big Ben, the hour bell of the Great Clock of Westminster, whose chimes or 'bongs' later became inextricably linked with ITN's *News at Ten*, celebrated its hundredth birthday. There was a special ceremony in Palace Yard, Westminster – all the party leaders were there. There was also an exhibition at Westminster throughout the summer at which MPs and members of the public could see Charles Barry's original designs. The name, it was reported, was derived from that of Sir Benjamin Hall, a large and ponderous man who was Chief Lord of the Woods and Forests, and given to delivering very long and 'wooden' speeches. His nickname was 'Big Ben'. At the end of his contribution to the debate on the naming of the bell, a wag in the Chamber is said to have called out 'Why not call it Big Ben and have done with it!'

Above: Mr Charles King was responsible for winding Big Ben's clock and regulating the mechanism so it kept perfect time – by placing old pre-decimal pennies on the pendulum to slow it down or removing them if it needed speeding up.

Above: In April Big Ben celebrated its hundredth birthday – the mechanism driving the clock that set the time for Britain had been installed in 1859 and was still going strong.

Britain's first motorway, the M1, opens

Explorer VI sends first picture of Earth from space

Hawaii becomes 50th US State

Mau Mau leader Dedan Kimathi is arrested in Kenya

16 August

21 August

21 October

6 November

1960s

The sixties revolution was about pop music, politics and protest. But at ITN, television news was changing too. Colour made news footage even more arresting and ITN pioneered the on-the-spot report. Reporters were no longer a disembodied voice-over – ITN viewers saw them in the field. Satellite transmissions meant ITN viewers could see on-the-day pictures of what was happening thousands of miles away – sometimes even as they happened. As the curtains in front of our window on the world were pulled back, *News at Ten* was launched. Britain's first half hour news programme was something the public wanted to watch. Its ratings-winning performance proved that.

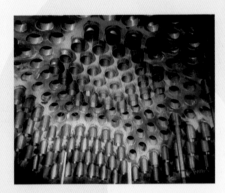

Above left: Inside the Windscale Atomic Energy plant, a worker checks inside the top of the pressure vessel of the new gas-cooled reactor.

Above middle: View of inside of the top dome of the pressure vessel, showing the stubs through which the fuel elements will be charged and discharged

Above right: Overall view of the new Windscale plant, which was being built in Cumberland.

Above: President Eisenhower meets President-elect John F Kennedy at the White House.

Atomic weapons and atomic power dominated the news at the start of the decade. The two Superpowers, the United States and the Soviet Union, were trying to agree limits on the proliferation of atomic weapons, test ban treaties and even nuclear disarmament. Both President Eisenhower and his young successor, John F Kennedy, held talks with the Soviet leader, Nikita Khrushchev.

While they were doing so, Gary Powers, the pilot of an American Lockheed U2 'high-altitude reconnaissance aircraft', more commonly referred to as a spy-plane, was shot down near Svedlovsk in the Soviet Union. He had been photographing missile sites, but the Americans maintained that the plane was conducting weather observations – taking pictures of the clouds. The incident caused much acrimony between Russia and America. Powers was tried – very publicly – in Moscow and sentenced to 10 years imprisonment. ITN interviewed his parents at Heathrow Airport, as they flew from the United States to Moscow for the trial. Less than two years later, in one of the most dramatic episodes of the Cold War, he was exchanged, in the middle of a bridge linking East and West Berlin over the river Havel, for Colonel Rudolf Abel, a Soviet 'master spy'.

Nigella Lawson, celebrity chef, is born

France explodes its first atomic bomb

Prince Andrew is born

The Sharpeville Massacre

6 January

13 February

19 February

21 March

The peaceful use of atomic power continued in Britain. Despite a devastating leak at Windscale nuclear plant in Cumbria three years earlier, work by the UK Atomic Energy Authority was progressing on an advanced gas-cooled atomic reactor there – a proto-type of larger reactors to come. The new reactor was to be operational the following year. The Government said the new design offered a 'considerable reduction' in the cost of producing nuclear power.

In South Africa, 1960 will be remembered for the worst atrocity of the apartheid era. 70 unarmed protesters were killed in the Sharpeville massacre, in the Transvaal. A protest had been held there against the Pass Law – which required non-whites to carry identification papers at all times. If anyone was caught without their pass, they could be imprisoned indefinitely, without trial, in solitary confinement, and without access to either their family or a lawyer. 5,000 people took part in the demonstration; the police managed to disperse almost all of them but 300 remained. When they refused to go, the police opened fire, even on those who were running away. ITN showed images of bodies strewn across the street that shocked the world but the South African government's reaction was simply to ban all non-white political organisations, including Nelson Mandela's African National Congress. In the days that followed, ITN also reported the funerals of the victims and a protest march through London, that ended with a rally in Trafalgar Square.

There were also problems in another part of Africa – the Congo, now the Democratic Republic of Congo. Within weeks of gaining independence from Belgium, the country was plunged into violence as a variety of individuals and factions vied for control of a chaotic – and Soviet supported – regime.

Above left: Refugees in Northern Rhodesia now Zimbabwe, after riots and violence had driven them from their homes in the Congo.

Above right: Many refugees were armed, even small children – this massive collection of guns and other weapons was collected from them after they arrived from Rhodesia.

Above: A victim of the notorious Sharpeville Massacre.

Elvis releases his single, 'Are You Lonesome Tonight?'

U2 spy plane shot down by Soviet missile and Gary Powers captured

Princess Margaret marries Anthony Armstrong-Jones

At the Paris Summit, Khrushchev demands an apology from President Eisenhower for the U2 incident

4 April

1 May

6 May

16 May

Above: The wedding of Princess Margaret, younger sister of Queen Elizabeth II, to Anthony Armstrong-Jones was the society event of 1960.

Above: The happy couple leave for their honeymoon. The hat the Princess is wearing was quickly copied and became that season's must-have, worn by young and old alike.

Without question, the society wedding of the year was the marriage of Princess Margaret, Queen Elizabeth's younger sister, to photographer Anthony Armstrong-Jones on May 6th.

The Queen's eldest daughter, Princess Anne, was Maid of Honour. The happy couple honeymooned in the West Indies. ITN covered the wedding and throughout the rest of the year filmed their various glamorous public appearances at film premieres and theatre first nights.

Above: Princess Margaret and Anthony Armstrong-Jones – later Lord Snowdon – pose together for photographers.

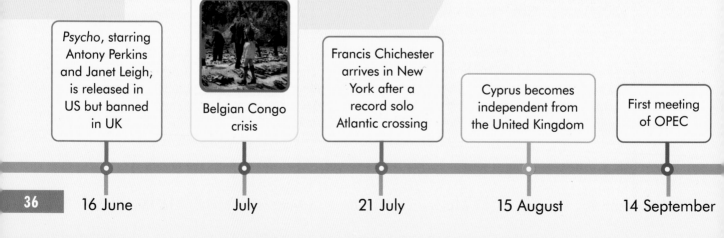

Psycho, starring Antony Perkins and Janet Leigh, is released in US but banned in UK

Belgian Congo crisis

Francis Chichester arrives in New York after a record solo Atlantic crossing

Cyprus becomes independent from the United Kingdom

First meeting of OPEC

16 June   July   21 July   15 August   14 September

The Queen's second son, Prince Andrew, was born but didn't make his first public appearance until he was seven months old. ITN cameras were in Balmoral, in September, as the Queen and Duke of Edinburgh proudly showed him off, alongside his elder brother and sister.

Fashion in 1960 was beginning to take its lead from London rather than Paris or Milan. The era of Mary Quant was dawning. OPEC met for the first time, in a tent. *Lady Chatterley's Lover* went on sale – ITN cameras filmed the queues outside a bookshop in Leicester Square, then inside the piles of books and an assistant shouting 'One copy only, thank you'. An unknown young American boxer Cassius Clay – later Muhammad Ali – won a gold medal at the Rome Olympics. The contraceptive pill became available and the sexual revolution was born.

Above: Winklepickers were all the rage with both men and women – despite the damage the sharply-pointed toes must have been doing to tender young feet.

Above: The fashion-conscious man-about-town still wore a hat – and London stores had a wide range of men's hats for every occasion for him to choose from.

Left: In the days before wearing real fur was considered environmentally unsound, a model (far left) wears a ranch mink coat, priced at £2,850. The model on the right is wearing a full-length silk taffeta evening dress – which retailed at the princely sum of £12 1s 6d.

Nixon and Kennedy participate in the first televised presidential debate

Khruschev addresses the UN to protest about discussion of Soviet policy towards Eastern Europe

Penguin books is found not guilty of obscenity in the *Lady Chatterley's Lover* case. The book becomes a best seller

John F Kennedy elected President of the US

26 September

12 October

2 November

8 November

Above: Queen Elizabeth II is driven through the streets of Karachi in an open-topped car with President Ayub Khan.

Above: The Queen smiles as she meets the ladies of Karachi, many dressed in colourful saris and probably more comfortable than Her Highness in the searing heat.

Above: After visiting the North West Frontier and Lahore, the Queen and Prince Philip arrived in Bombay.

The Queen and Prince Philip went on a tour of India and Pakistan in February, visiting what had been, in the then not-so-distant days of Empire, the North West Frontier. The Royal Tour was the subject of intense interest and ITN was there. It covered the serious parts of the tour, such as the Queen's speech in New Delhi, talking of her hope that the visit would demonstrate respect and friendship. But it also reported the more colourful moments, including the royal couple riding elephants to a civic reception in Jaipur and a visit by the Queen and Prince to the Taj Mahal.

Above: During her visit to the North West Frontier, Queen Elizabeth II meets the Malak chiefs, who presented her with a sheep.

On the morning of August 13th, Berliners awoke to discover that their city was divided – literally. During the night, East German troops had sealed the border with barbed wire, including road and rail links, trapping hundreds on the wrong side and preventing many more from getting to work. Churchill's 'Iron Curtain' had become a reality. Work began immediately on the construction of a concrete wall. Eventually, two walls were constructed, each four metres high and separated by a lethal no-man's land in which many died in desperate attempts to reach the West. The Berlin Wall remained the most potent symbol of the Cold War until it came crashing down in 1989.

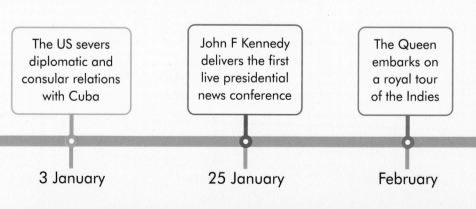

The US severs diplomatic and consular relations with Cuba

John F Kennedy delivers the first live presidential news conference

The Queen embarks on a royal tour of the Indies

3 January

25 January

February

Barbara Mandell

Barbara Mandell was the first woman ever to read the news on British television. Her debut was at 12pm on ITN's first lunchtime bulletin on September 23rd, 1955. She had already gained considerable experience as a broadcaster in South Africa. Putting her in the midday bulletin on the first full day of broadcasting sent a clear message to viewers used to the gentlemen of the BBC that ITN was in the business of innovation, not imitation. The daytime news slot was subsequently dropped as an economy measure and Ms. Mandell transferred to reporting and to reading the news at weekends. Her report on the *Heartbreak Special* – a train that carried children to Liverpool en route to Canada and, hopefully, a better life – made a profound impression on those who saw it: an early and powerful example of the 'human interest' story that television news could put across so effectively.

Above: Nepalese children in Katmandu wave Union Jacks as they wait to see their royal visitor.

Above: During her trip to Pakistan, the Queen visited the Badshahi Mosque in Lahore.

But the biggest story of 1961 was literally out of the world – the landing of the very first man on the moon, a Russian called Yuri Gagarin.

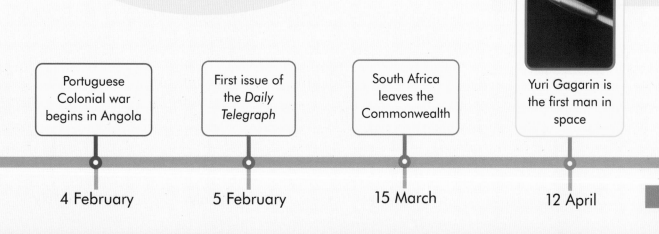

Portuguese Colonial war begins in Angola	First issue of the *Daily Telegraph*	South Africa leaves the Commonwealth	Yuri Gagarin is the first man in space
4 February	5 February	15 March	12 April

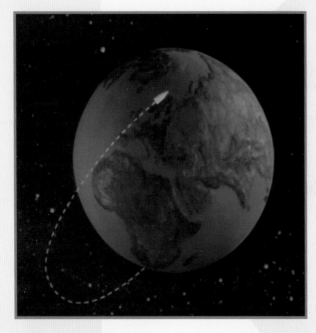

Above: Gagarin's ship, Vostok I, reached a height of 188 miles and orbited the Earth. His first words were 'I see Earth! It's so beautiful!' – but in Russian, of course.

Above: Russian cosmonaut Yuri Gagarin, the first man in space.

People of the world! Let us safeguard and enhance this beauty, not destroy it… Yuri Gagarin

On the morning of April 12th, Soviet Cosmonaut Yuri Alexeyevitch Gagarin was driven out to the launch site at Baikonur in Kazakhstan, along with backup pilot Gherman Titov. He was helped aboard *Vostok 1* and, at just after 9am, was launched into space, reaching an altitude just short of 188 miles and a speed of 18,000 miles per hour. Gagarin became the first human being in history actually to see that our planet is a sphere and that most of it is covered with water. The first words from space were, 'I see Earth! It's so beautiful!'

Gagarin's promotion was almost as rapid as the speed of his capsule: he went up a Senior Lieutenant and came down a Major and a hero of the Soviet Union. He landed in a potato field, clambered out and, in his bright orange suit, managed to frighten an old lady who asked him if he'd come from space.

Gagarin's flight was, by any standards, a big story and ITN rose to the occasion. Peter Fairley, a reporter for London's *Evening Standard* newspaper, had been interviewed by ITN's *Dateline* programme and demonstrated a remarkable knowledge of both the Soviet Union's and the United States' space programmes, having made a detailed study of the subject dating from the launch of Russia's *Sputnik 1* in 1957. Crucially, Fairley was able to put across technical information in a manner that rendered it accessible without detracting from its inherent excitement. He was quickly appointed Science Correspondent at ITN and continued to cover the Space Race throughout the sixties, including providing unforgettable coverage of the first moon landings in 1969.

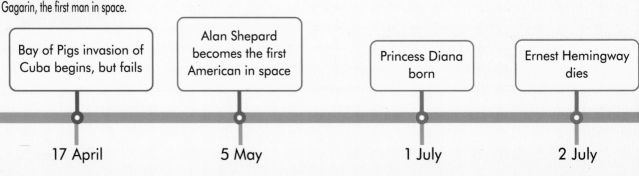

Bay of Pigs invasion of Cuba begins, but fails

Alan Shepard becomes the first American in space

Princess Diana born

Ernest Hemingway dies

17 April

5 May

1 July

2 July

Two days after Gargarin's famous and historic voyage, ITN covered the hero's welcome he was given in Moscow's Red Square. Later in the year, in July, ITN also covered Yuri Gagarin's visit to Britain. He was driven from Heathrow Airport in an open top Rolls Royce with the registration plate YG1, through cheering crowds to the Soviet Embassy in central London. Later he was invited to Buckingham Palace to meet the royal family, to a reception with UK Prime Minister Harold Macmillan and was presented with a medal by the Foundry Workers' Union in Manchester.

Above: The Americans were not having quite such luck with their space programme. The Atlas rocket taking a space capsule up failed just after launch, and the mission had to be aborted by controllers. The rocket was blown up, but the space capsule returned safely to earth.

Above: Sailors on the *USS Randolph* watch the space capsule of NASA astronaut 'Gus' Grissom come down into the sea.

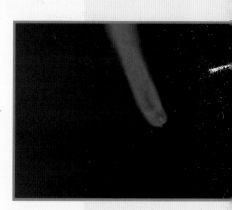

Above: Grissom returns to earth – he was the third man in space.

Gus Grissom becomes the third man in space in *Liberty Bell 7*

Start of construction of the Berlin Wall

US troops arrive in Vietnam

21 July

13 August

11 December

1962 America

Above and right: Astronaut John Glenn, the first American to orbit the Earth, meets US President John F Kennedy. After the meeting, Kennedy vowed the Americans would put a man on the moon...

Above: While America dreamed dreams, Britain was suffering gale force winds that whipped the sea to crash against the shore along the south coast.

Although they may not have realised it, the most significant event of the year for ITN viewers was the launch, on July 10th, of the American Telstar satellite. From that day onwards, television pictures could be beamed across the Atlantic. Suddenly events in the United States didn't seem thousands of miles away. They could be broadcast the day they happened – they could even be shown live. Before satellites, film had to be flown back to London by plane which meant the pictures were usually broadcast a day after they had been shot. The new satellite technology brought an immediacy that captured the viewers' imagination.

The space race itself was now hotting up as the United States was quick to respond to the Soviet Union's progress. Astronaut John Glenn, born in Cambridge, Ohio, was a veteran fighter pilot, having served in World War II and in Korea. In 1957 he had piloted the first supersonic transcontinental

Pope John XXIII excommunicates Fidel Castro

Eisenhower visits Disneyland

Heavy floods around Hamburg

John Glenn becomes first American to orbit the Earth

3 January

4 January

16–17 Febraury

20 February

flight and then in February 1962, he orbited the earth in *Friendship 7*, becoming the first American to do so. Glenn went on to be elected to the US Senate and, in 1998, became the oldest man to fly in space, aboard the Space Shuttle *Discovery*. He was 77. After his 1962 flight, Glenn was received by President John F Kennedy who vowed that America would put a man on the moon by the end of the decade. To achieve this, he asked Congress to grant US$ 2 billion to the Apollo programme, and they did.

Back down on earth, President Kennedy faced the Cuba Missile Crisis, which was largely, if not entirely, a consequence of his ill-advised involvement in the Bay of Pigs invasion the previous year. This had been intended to remove the Soviet sympathising Fidel Castro from power by landing a force of 1,500 Cuban exiles, trained and armed by the US military, at the Bay of Pigs on Cuba's south coast. The invasion failed, to the immense embarrassment of the United States. Castro was driven closer to Russia, offering the Soviets the opportunity to build missile bases on Cuba which lies only 90 miles from Key West in Florida.

On October 16th, 1962, President Kennedy learned that a U2 spy plane had photographed missile sites under construction on Cuba. Within a week he had informed the world's media, characterising Russia's actions as, 'deliberately provocative and unjustified…' He followed this up by ordering a naval blockade to try to halt a convoy of 20 Russian ships carrying missiles and escorted by two Soviet Navy submarines. US warships took up station, the Russian flotilla steamed on and the world held its breath.

Threat of a nuclear holocaust loomed. The two mighty Superpowers had squared up to each other and stood eye-to-eye then, as Dean Rusk, the US Secretary of State put it 'the other fella blinked'. The Russian ships slowed and stopped – and then turned for home. Khrushchev agreed to dismantle his Cuban bases on condition that the United States guaranteed that it would not attempt again to invade the island.

Above: America also suffered its share of bad weather – in June a tornado hit Connecticut, wrecking 300 homes.

Above: As well as their homes, many also lost their cars – either crushed beneath falling trees, or just picked up and smashed by the wind.

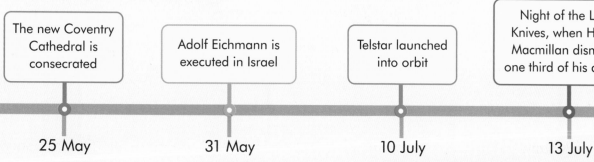

The new Coventry Cathedral is consecrated

Adolf Eichmann is executed in Israel

Telstar launched into orbit

Night of the Long Knives, when Harold Macmillan dismisses one third of his cabinet

25 May   31 May   10 July   13 July

Above: Former President Eisenhower takes a break with his family and visits Disneyland in California. Although he was no longer in power, Ike was still immensely popular and was followed around the park by the ever-present newsmen. He clowned around for the cameras, putting on a fireman's helmet and riding in a vintage car. At the end of his visit he watched one of the famous Disney parades.

Right: Jack Warner, head of Warner Brothers, with Marilyn Monroe.

Far right: Marilyn poses with her third husband, playwright Arthur Miller.

The big attraction at Disneyland in California in 1962 was former President Eisenhower. Two years after leaving office he was still a popular figure and was mobbed by reporters during his visit. The world's first theme park had opened in 1955 and one of the compères at the opening ceremony was a film actor called Ronald Reagan.

Still in the United States, 1962 saw the untimely death of one of Hollywood's most iconic stars, Marilyn Monroe. Marilyn, whose behaviour had become increasingly erratic, was fired from George Cukor's *Something's*

Marilyn Monroe dies from an overdose

First Beatles single, 'Love Me Do', is released

Pope John XXIII convenes Vatican II

5 August

5 October

11 October

Left: An AA patrolman arrives to help a stranded motorist, caught in the Big Freeze that hit Britain in late 1962.

Got To Give for persistent absence. In the small hours of the morning of August 5th, her housekeeper, Eunice Murray, noticed that Marilyn's light was on. The bedroom door was locked so Eunice had to peep through the window to see her, lying face down on her bed, with the phone in her hand and an almost empty bottle of sleeping tablets beside her.

Left: Two-year-old Mary Crosby, daughter of American crooner Bing Crosby, gets an early taste of life in front of the camera as she wins a swimming certificate. Later she achieved world-wide fame as the person who shot JR in Dallas!

Cuban Missile Crisis begins, when a spy plane takes pictures of Soviet nuclear weapons being installed

Lawrence of Arabia, starring Omar Sharif and Peter O'Toole, is released

The Big Freeze begins in Britain, with no frost-free nights until March 5th

14 October

10 December

22 December

Above: Thousands march from Aldermaston to London to protest at the Houses of Parliament. The men chanted 'Tories out!' or raised their arms in Nazi-style salutes.

Above: Police on foot and on horseback try to prevent the protestors from storming the seat of British government.

Just over a week after becoming an ITN reporter, Gerald Seymour was assigned to what the tabloids would call 'The Crime of the Century'. The Great Train Robbery was a big time crime perpetrated by small time criminals. At 3.15am on August 8th, the Glasgow to Euston mail train was stopped by a bogus red light near Cheddington in Buckinghamshire. A gang of thieves boarded the train and uncoupled the first two coaches, which they then had driven to a rendezvous point at a bridge only a mile down the track. Here they broke into the second carriage, tied up the four postal workers inside and made off with sacks of money totalling over £2.5 million. The driver of the train, Jack Mills, received severe head injuries and was never able to return to work. Following a massive police operation, the gang's abandoned hideout was discovered at Leatherslade Farm in Bedfordshire. Within six months, 12 of the gang's 15 members had been apprehended, tried and sentenced to a total of over 300 years imprisonment. Bruce Reynolds, an antique dealer and thief who was believed to have been the 'mastermind' behind the operation evaded capture until 1969, when he was finally sentenced to 10 years in jail. Ronald Biggs and Charlie Wilson managed a daring escape from Winson Green Prison in Birmingham. Biggs surfaced in Rio de Janeiro, a sad figure, trading on his dubious reputation by having his photograph taken with tourists to make a few dollars. He returned, sick, to Britain in 2001 for medical treatment and was finally imprisoned. Charlie Wilson was traced to a Montreal suburb, moved to the Costa del Sol in Spain, became involved in drug trafficking and was shot by an assassin, in his swimming pool, in 1990.

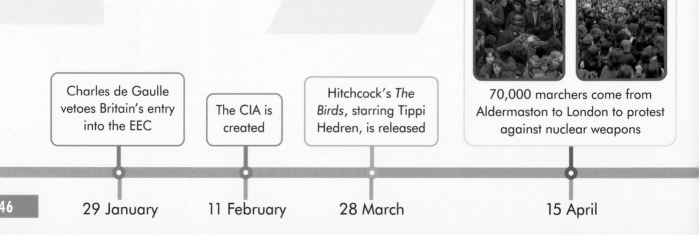

70,000 marchers come from Aldermaston to London to protest against nuclear weapons

Charles de Gaulle vetoes Britain's entry into the EEC

The CIA is created

Hitchcock's *The Birds*, starring Tippi Hedren, is released

29 January

11 February

28 March

15 April

Sandy Gall CBE

Sandy Gall was born in 1927 in Penang, Malaysia, the son of a rubber planter. He attended Glenalmond School in Scotland and graduated from Aberdeen University. He joined Reuters in 1953 and, a decade later, moved to ITN, where he was their first reporter to deliver despatches from Vietnam. At the end of the conflict, as everyone else was leaving, he elected to stay on to cover the fall of Saigon with a French camera crew. He served as a newscaster on *News at Ten* for 20 years, but in 1982 reverted to war reporting with a trip to Afghanistan, producing detailed reports and three full-length documentaries. He established the Afghanistan Appeal charity in 1983. In 1991, Sandy Gall was the first Western journalist to report live from Kuwait, within hours of the launch of the start of its liberation by allied forces. He was awarded the CBE in 1988.

Above: Muhammad Ali predicts that Henry Cooper will fall in the fifth round, at the weigh-in before their fight at Wembley in June 1963. Cooper was indeed knocked out in the fifth.

Above: Ladies in the 1960s were still concerned about looking perfect at all times – the natural look was definitely not in. This woman is swimming with full make-up...

Above: ... but when she comes out of the water she whips off her blonde hair to reveal that it is actually a nylon swimming cap.

John Profumo resigns in a sex scandal involving Christine Keeler and Mandy Rice-Davies

Pope John XXIII dies, succeeded by Pope Paul VI

Russians put first woman, Valentine Tereshkova, into space

3 June

5 June

16 June

Above left: The assassination of President John F Kennedy, live on camera. Jackie and the President wave to crowds on the streets of Dallas as their motorcade passes...

Above middle: ...The car moves on...

Above right: ... a few seconds later shots ring out. The President was rushed to hospital in Dallas, but was pronounced dead shortly afterwards.

The world was stunned by the assassination of President Kennedy on Friday November 22nd. It was – despite the magnitude of the story – one that was initially very difficult to cover.

News came through in the evening in London, when ITV was on air with *Emergency Ward 10*. Breaking into a network, with different regional broadcasters, to provide a newsflash took several minutes and no pictures were available in London. ITN ran an extended news bulletin at 9pm and a filmed obituary that had been prepared in advance to cover just such a terrible eventuality. The cine film of the assassination itself, shot by amateur cameraman Abraham Zapruder, took a few days to emerge.

The President had been hit by bullets fired by Lee Harvey Oswald from a window on the third floor of the Texas school book depository while driving

Muhammad Ali fights Henry Cooper for the first time at Wembley Stadium and knocks him out in the fifth round

Kennedy visits Berlin: 'Ich bin ein Berliner...'

The US, UK and USSR sign a nuclear test ban treaty

18 June

26 June

5 August

in a motorcade through Dallas, Texas. The President was rushed to the Parkland Memorial Hospital but was pronounced dead half an hour later.

Winston Churchill summed up the thoughts of many in Britain, describing the assassination as a 'monstrous act that has taken from us a great statesman and a valiant man'. Conspiracy theories have abounded about whether Oswald really was the killer and if so, whether he acted alone. He was an ex-US marine, married to a Russian woman he had met in Minsk.

While the world was still absorbing the shock, there was another dramatic development on the Sunday evening. Oswald was shot dead by Jack Ruby while being escorted through Dallas police station – and American television cameras filmed it live.

President Kennedy's funeral was held on the Monday. His burial in Arlington cemetery took place at a time of the day when the Telstar satellite was able to beam live pictures to Europe, where America's grief was shared. It was perhaps fitting that television could mark, in this way, the end of the life of the first new leader of the television age.

Above left: President John F Kennedy's coffin lying in state in the White House, draped with the American flag.

Above middle: At the funeral, the President's widow, Jacqueline Kennedy, heavily veiled, stands with her children Caroline and John Junior, and her brothers-in-law, Robert and Edward Kennedy.

Above right: The Stars and Stripes that covered the coffin is folded up by the servicemen flag bearers, before being handed to Jacqueline Kennedy.

Above: Happier days – President John F Kennedy inspects the troops during a visit to Ireland earlier that year.

Great Train Robbery, in Buckinghamshire

Martin Luther King makes his 'I have a dream' speech at the end of the march on Washington

President Kennedy assassinated

Civil war erupts in Cyprus

8 August

28 August

22 November

24 December

1964 Beatlemania

Beatlemania reached America – and the Fab Four were mobbed by fans when they arrived in New York. Their first appearance on *The Ed Sullivan Show* was watched by an audience estimated at over 70 million. 'Please Please Me' went to Number One in the US charts and 'Can't Buy Me Love' subsequently became the first single to be Number 1 in both the US and the UK. It seemed the Mersey beat had crossed the Atlantic. When The Beatles flew back to Heathrow airport they were mobbed all over again.

ITN's *Roving Report* was to follow their last tour to the US in 1966, picking up on John Lennon's infamous observation that The Beatles were 'bigger

Below left: On their return to Heathrow after conquering America, the Fab Four stop on the steps of the plane to survey the vast crowd that has gathered to meet them.

Below right: Beatlemania in action: Every time The Beatles were expected, Heathrow was swamped with hysterical teenagers desperate for a glimpse of their favourite group.

Cuba buys 450 buses from British Leyland in defiance of the US trade ban

'I Want To Hold Your Hand' is released in the US and becomes The Beatles' first US hit

Dr. Strangelove, starring Peter Sellers, is released

7 January

13 January

29 January

than Jesus', with a film entitled *The Beatles in the Bible Belt,* following the band through the Southern 'Bible Belt' states to gauge reaction. Protests were staged, records were burned – and a great piece of television was produced.

Beatlemania may have been in the news on both sides of the Atlantic, but the real story of 1964 was America's entry into war in Vietnam following an attack on an American destroyer, the *USS Maddox,* in the Gulf of Tonkin. Over the next decade nearly 50,000 Americans and a million Vietnamese would die in a war that was brought, by television, into living rooms across the world.

Below left: Paul, Ringo, George and John face the cameras at a press conference in JFK Airport on their arrival in New York.

Below right: Teenagers holding banners – the text based on a recent Beatles' hit – hoping to catch the eye of one of the boys.

The Beatles arrive in New York to conquer America

Muhammad Ali beats Sonny Liston to become Heavyweight Champion of the World

Prince Edward is born

Richard Burton marries Liz Taylor for the first time

7 February

25 February

10 March

15 March

Above and right: The Forth Road Bridge was the longest suspension bridge in Europe, when it opened in September 1964. It replaced a ferry that had operated across the Firth of Forth, but drivers had to pay a toll to use it.

After 40 years in the planning, the Forth Road Bridge was opened by the Queen on September 4th. There had been a railway bridge across the Firth of Forth since 1890, but when it was opened, the one-and-a-half mile road link was the longest suspension bridge in Europe and the fourth longest in the world. The bridge had been shrouded in mist early in the day

Above: Queen Elizabeth II makes a speech as she opens the bridge.

Above: The Queen walks down with the Duke of Edinburgh to take the last ferry journey across the Firth of Forth.

Above: A plaque set in stone was placed on either side of the bridge to record the opening ceremony.

The first pirate radio station, Radio Caroline, begins broadcasting

BBC2 launched

Nelson Mandela sentenced to life imprisonment

28 March

20 April

12 June

but cleared in time for the opening. However, the poor weather meant a fly-past by the RAF, just before the ceremony, had to be cancelled, but eight Royal Navy ships moored in the estuary gave the new bridge a 21 gun salute.

Britain's longest motorway, the M6, was extended into Cumbria. Seat belts were appearing as standard features on new cars, though their fitting and wearing were not compulsory. The motor car was beginning to dominate the British landscape, both physically and socially. Rising prosperity brought exciting new cars like the Mini within the purchasing power of those who would never have dreamed of owning a motor car a decade earlier.

Above: Car seat belts are tested at the British Standards Institute in Hemel Hempstead.

Above: Seat belts were not fitted to most cars as standard at this time, but there were already moves to make wearing them compulsory.

Left: Transport Minister Ernest Marples inspects work on the M6 motorway, which was being extended into Cumbria.

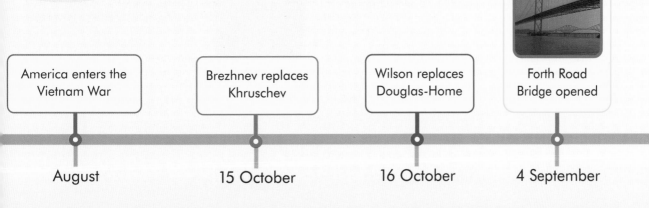

America enters the Vietnam War	Brezhnev replaces Khruschev	Wilson replaces Douglas-Home	Forth Road Bridge opened
August	15 October	16 October	4 September

The Royal Ocean Racing Club's premier competition, the Admiral's Cup, was contested at Cowes, Isle of Wight, by boats from Britain, Sweden, Holland, France, Ireland, Australia and the United States. In the Fastnet Race, the final event in the series, an innovative new 34 foot sloop, *Rabbit*, won in its class and helped to ensure British victory overall.

Above: In the Sydney-Hobart yacht race the schooner *Astor* arrived home first, but the sloop *Freya* – which actually came in third – won on handicap.

Legendary footballer Sir Stanley Matthews, who had been knighted the previous year, retired at the age of 50. He played his last game five days after his birthday. Some of Europe's top players turned out for his testimonial match at Stoke City. His career had spanned 33 years and he had made over 700 appearances for Stoke City and Blackpool. Sir Stanley had played for England 54 times and for Great Britain twice. He was known variously as the Wizard of Dribble and the First Gentleman of Football – during his entire career he was never once booked by a referee. He died in 2000 and 100,000 fans turned out to pay their respects.

Racing driver Jim Clark became the first British winner of the Indianpolis 500. Former world heavy-weight boxing champion Freddie Mills was found shot dead in his car in Soho.

Above: Sir Stanley Matthews and athlete Mary Rand pose outside Buckingham Palace after being honoured by the Queen in 1964. Mary Rand had received the OBE and Stanley Matthews was knighted.

Prime Ministers of Northern Ireland and the Republic meet for the first time in 43 years

Winston Churchill dies

Churchill's funeral is watched by 350 million people worldwide

14 January

24 January

30 January

Reginald Bosanquet

"Reggie" Bosanquet was born in 1932, the son of a cricketer, B. J. T. Bosanquet – the inventor of the googly delivery in cricket. As a boy, during the war, he was evacuated to Canada and, on his return, was sent to Winchester College. From there, he went up to New College, Oxford. He applied to ITN for a job in 1955, straight from university, saying he wanted to be a star. He was told he could have a job as a tea-boy on £10 a week. He accepted and went on to become a sub-editor and then a reporter in 1957. He spent eight years presenting ITN's *Dateline* and became a newscaster on *News at Ten* at its launch in 1967. His natural charm, informal manner and air of mischief made him immensely popular with the viewers and stories of epic drinking bouts and outrageous off-screen behaviour only served to enhance his reputation. An attempt to remove him was countered by a successful *Hands off Reggie!* campaign in the Sunday papers. He raised the *And finally* spot to the level of an art form and his hair piece became an object of national fascination. He left ITN in 1979 and died in 1984 at the age of 51.

Above: A North London synchronised swimming team perform their routine at Butlin's Holiday Camp in Clacton, Essex.

Above: A competitor at the World Bobsleigh Championships, held at Davos in Switzerland in February 1965.

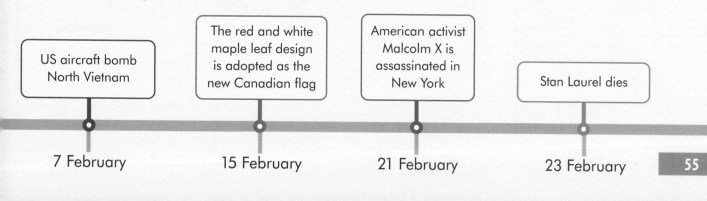

US aircraft bomb North Vietnam

The red and white maple leaf design is adopted as the new Canadian flag

American activist Malcolm X is assassinated in New York

Stan Laurel dies

7 February

15 February

21 February

23 February

Above: Views of the military procession that accompanied Sir Winston Churchill's coffin through the streets of London from Westminster Hall, where it had lain in State. It included sailors and soldiers with their rifles pointing downwards, a military band and the Royal Horseguards.

In January the British public waited for news of what appeared to be the impending death of Sir Winston Churchill. His doctor, Lord Moran, announced that he had suffered a cerebral stroke. ITN reporters were placed on round the clock rotation outside his house in Hyde Park, as his life looked to be slipping away. He was 90 years old. He'd already announced, on his 75th birthday, 'I am ready to meet my Maker. Whether my Maker is prepared for the ordeal of meeting me is another matter'.

Lord Moran kept reporters informed of his medical condition. ITN cameras filmed flowers arriving at Churchill's home and crowds gathering outside, waiting for news. Among the newspaper headlines, one read 'Winston weaker in his biggest battle'.

When the end came, ITN didn't just have to report his death and the huge reaction to it, but also had to provide a network documentary of his life. ITN did prepare obituaries of famous people but they were more usually for news bulletins. However, the documentary produced on the night of Churchill's death, January 24th, was nearly two hours long. It got good reviews and compared well with the BBC version, which was voiced by Sir Laurence Olivier. The *Television Today* magazine said, '...both channels did wonderfully well. ITN's version seemed to have the edge with intimacy and humour. Sir Winston always was a rebel with a puckish sense of humour, and somehow the ITV version put across the Churchillian chuckle, whereas the BBC's effort was more solemn'.

Churchill was the first politician to be given a state funeral. His lying in state at Westminster Hall lasted for three days. ITN cameras filmed the queues of people waiting to pay their respects and spoke to them about their memories of him during the Second World War. People were given hot drinks as they waited in the cold and by the time of his funeral, nearly a third of a million had filed past his coffin.

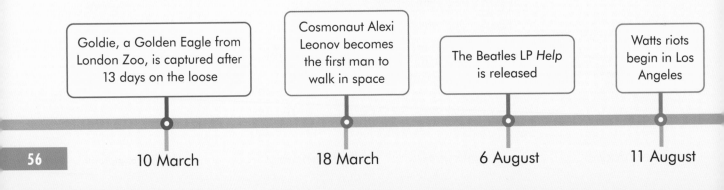

Goldie, a Golden Eagle from London Zoo, is captured after 13 days on the loose

Cosmonaut Alexi Leonov becomes the first man to walk in space

The Beatles LP *Help* is released

Watts riots begin in Los Angeles

10 March

18 March

6 August

11 August

Far left: Sailors of the Royal Navy draw the gun carriage that bears the coffin.

Left: The coffin on a plinth in St Paul's Cathedral, covered with a Union Jack. A host of international statesmen and royalty came to pay their respects to the great man.

As the funeral drew nearer, dignitaries from around the world began to arrive – first among them the former United States President Dwight Eisenhower, the Allies' Supreme Commander at the time of the D-Day landings that liberated Europe. He was joined by kings, presidents and prime ministers.

Around the country millions of people watched the live coverage. Factories came to a standstill and people were given the day off work. The funeral service was at St Paul's Cathedral. Churchill's body was carried there on a gun carriage. From the Cathedral, the coffin was taken, by motor launch, across the Thames to Waterloo station. As the launch passed, the dockyard cranes that still lined the Thames dipped their jibs in silent salute. More than all the pomp, the gun carriage and the muffled drums, this simple gesture by the dock workers brought home to many what it truly meant to be honoured. At Waterloo, the coffin was placed on a train for the journey to his final burial place, the village churchyard at Bladon, near the family estate at Blenheim.

Below: The streets were lined with thousands of ordinary people, who had been given the day off work and who came to mourn one of the world's great leaders.

Bob Dylan releases his first all-electric album, *Highway 61 Revisited*

Ian Smith declares Rhodesia, now called Zimbabwe, to be independent

de Gaulle re-elected

Doctor Zhivago, Starring Julie Christie and Omar Sharif, is released

30 August

11 November

5 December

22 December

1966 England Rules!

Above left: England and Germany fight it out – this time on the green grass of Wembley Stadium.

Above right: Bobby Moore is carried on the shoulders of his team mates as he holds the World Cup aloft to the cheering crowds.

England had gone World Cup mad long before the competition started, let alone after the famous victory. ITN had covered the build up – both the team news and the souvenir sales. Many of the t-shirts and hats featured a cuddly-looking lion called World Cup Willy.

ITN also reported the theft of the cup itself from a stamp exhibition in Central Hall in Westminster - stamps worth £3m were not touched. A nationwide hunt for the cup began but it wasn't until a week later that a mongrel dog called Pickles found it. The dog was sniffing round some bushes when its owner saw something suspicious wrapped in newspaper. ITN staged what now might be called a reconstruction, persuading Pickles' owner to take the dog back to the bushes to recreate the scene.

Once the competition started, England finished top of their group and reached the final against West Germany. The game was played at Wembley Stadium on July 30th before a capacity crowd of over 96,000. Haller scored for Germany after 13 minutes, but six minutes later Geoff Hurst equalized for England. With only 12 minutes of play remaining and the teams visibly

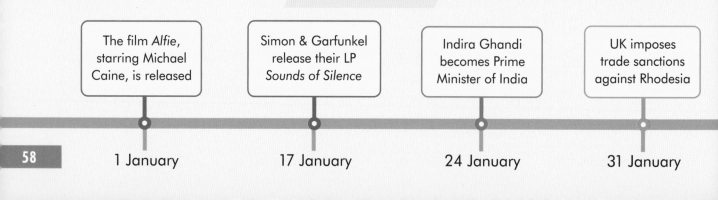

The film *Alfie*, starring Michael Caine, is released

1 January

Simon & Garfunkel release their LP *Sounds of Silence*

17 January

Indira Ghandi becomes Prime Minister of India

24 January

UK imposes trade sanctions against Rhodesia

31 January

tiring, Martin Peters put England ahead and the match – and the Jules Rimet Trophy – appeared to be theirs, but… Wolfgang Weber scored, right on the final whistle, and the game went to extra time – for the first time since 1934. In the 100th minute, Hurst powered a shot into the German goal mouth. The ball struck the underside of the bar, ricocheted down on to the ground and ran out. Had it crossed the line? All the world wondered… the Swiss referee, Gottfried Dienst, was unsure, but the Russian linesman, Tofik Bakhamarov, was in no doubt: it was a goal. The Germans protested. The match appeared to have been won, but would a famous victory be tarnished by dispute? No! Bobby Moore made a long pass to Geoff Hurst who put it unequivocally into the back of the German goal, even as spectators started to run on to the pitch, thus becoming the first player ever to score a hat-trick in a World Cup final. Bobby Moore climbed the stairs to the royal box and after carefully wiping his hands on the fabric decorating the box, he received the cup from the Queen.

Above: It was not only on the sports field that Britain was leading the way – Mary Quant was breaking new ground in the world of fashion.

Above: The famous mini, as seen on the catwalk rather than our roads – Mary Quant fashions were in demand all round the world.

At Arsenal's Highbury ground in North London, a crowd of 40,000 watched British boxer Henry Cooper attempt to wrest the World Heavyweight Championship from America's Muhammad Ali. Cooper fought valiantly but Ali landed two massive right handed punches to Cooper's head and opened up a deep cut over the left eye which required 12 stitches to close it. After the fight, Ali – who had recently changed his name from Cassius Clay after converting to Islam – visited Cooper in his dressing room and proclaimed, 'I hate to spill blood, it is against my religion…'

Left: Henry Cooper in training for his World Heavyweight contest against champion Muhammad Ali.

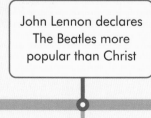

John Lennon declares The Beatles more popular than Christ

Labour Party under Harold Wilson wins the General Election

The State Opening of Parliament is televised for the first time

4 March

31 March

21 April

Above: The famous mini, as seen on our roads rather than the catwalk.

Right: Designed by Alec Issigonis, the little car had immediate appeal that transcended wealth and class. In 1969 it was the true star of *The Italian Job*, which also featured Michael Caine.

The big on-off romance of the year was covered in dozens of ITN reports. It didn't involve royalty or movie stars, but a female giant panda called Chi Chi. In an attempt to produce cubs in captivity, she was paired off with An An – a male giant panda in Moscow Zoo. Chi Chi had been a goodwill present from China in 1958. With tongues firmly in cheeks, ITN reporters covered the story as though it involved two people. The first report on the subject said Chi Chi was 'to be married at last'. She was filmed, heading off to Moscow Zoo. Next, she was shown in quarantine, displaying what were said to be 'pre-wedding nerves'. The 'wedding date', their first meeting, had to be postponed because the director of Moscow Zoo had 'flu. The 'Chi Chi meets An An' report on March 26th was quickly

Muhammad Ali defends his World Heavyweight title against Henry Cooper and wins in the 6th round

US puts an unmanned spacecraft, *Surveyor 1*, on the moon

England beat West Germany to win the World Cup

21 May

2 June

30 July

Far left: Chi Chi the panda starts her journey to Moscow, where everyone hoped she would produce a host of little pandas.

Left: The Panda Special – a BEA Vanguard – transported Chi Chi in comfort to her destination.

followed by 'Chi Chi splits up with An An' four days later. By September ITN reported that they 'were still good friends'. There was a reconciliation in October. They even spent a night together. But it didn't work out. The romance was at an end. Chi Chi returned home from Russia …*without* love.

British technology also made news: the Vickers VC10 jet airliner was demonstrated at the Farnborough Air Show and entered service with the Royal Air Force as a transport aircraft and later as a tanker for in-flight refuelling. Almost 40 years on, the VC10 is still in service and 19 are based at RAF Brize Norton in Oxfordshire.

On the ground, Alec Issigonis's mini car proved to be as much a symbol of the swinging sixties as the mini skirt, transcending class barriers with its combination of practicality and chic. Issigonis had a hand in the design of the Morris Minor. But his real success came when his bosses at the British Motor Corporation asked him to design an even smaller car that could still seat four people and use an existing engine.

Above: Aviator Sheila Scott returns to a heroine's welcome at London Airport after her record-breaking round the World flight.

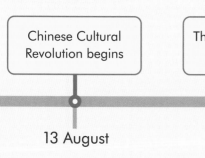

Chinese Cultural Revolution begins

The Severn Bridge is completed

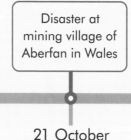

Disaster at mining village of Aberfan in Wales

Walt Disney dies

13 August

8 September

21 October

15 December

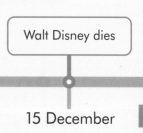

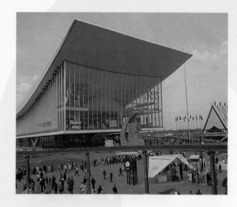

Above: A flavour of Expo '67: Top row, from left, the opening ceremony; the Russian Pavilion with its sweeping roof; the inverted pyramid of the Canadian Pavilion. Bottom row, from left: giant sculptures by Mario Armengol inside the British Pavilion; people enjoying a ride in the Expo Fairground; the Canadian Pulp and Paper Industry Pavilion.

Royal tours were by now establishing themselves as a regular part of ITN bulletins. With the longer airtime that *News at Ten* provided there was the chance to show more of events such as the Queen's visit to Canada, for Expo '67. It was held in Montreal to mark the centenary of Canada's confederation but it was a true world fair, exhibiting the best of international engineering and design. There were a hundred pavilions, representing nations, industries and 'themes' like *Man and His World*, plus a massive amusement park that featured a giant roller coaster called *Le Monstere*. Expo '67 attracted 50 million visitors and Alfa Romeo produced a new coupé – the Montreal – to commemorate the event.

Elvis marries Priscilla

Britain and Ireland apply to join the EEC

The Beatles release their LP *Sgt Pepper*

Barclays opens first cash machine

1 May

11 May

1 June

27 June

Left: The catastrophic oil spill from the stricken *Torrey Canyon* caused havoc among the wildlife on both sides of the Channel.

Other major items of news in 1967 included a catastrophic oil spill off the Cornish coast. The Liberian registered tanker *Torrey Canyon* had run aground on Pollard's Rock in the Seven Stones Reef between the Isles of Scilly and Land's End. Over 100,000 tons of crude oil leaked into the sea, causing major damage to marine and bird life along the Normandy coastline and along the South of England. Eventually, the stricken ship was bombed by aircraft of the Royal Air Force and the Fleet Air Arm in an attempt to burn the oil off the surface of the sea.

From the entertainment world came reports that Elvis had married Priscilla Beaulieu in a ceremony in Las Vegas. She had been his constant companion for more than three years, but had been kept out of the spotlight. Despite their apparent happiness in wedding pictures, the marriage was to last less than four years. Also from America came The Monkees, who arrived in 1967 to tour the UK. The group had been formed to appear in a TV series of the same name about the antics of a wacky pop group, but their music had unexpectedly become hugely popular, so they began touring and performing live.

Above: Priscilla and Elvis Presley on their wedding day in Las Vegas. The short ceremony itself was a private affair, but afterwards the bride and groom held a press conference in the Aladdin Hotel.

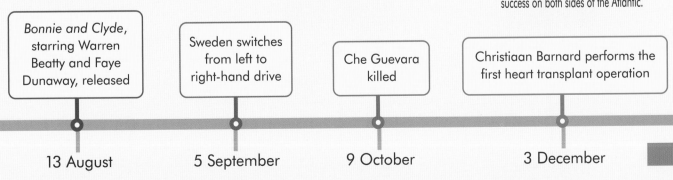

Above: The Monkees hit Britain. They were already well known here, as their American TV series was also shown in Britain and their records had been a tremendous success on both sides of the Atlantic.

Bonnie and Clyde, starring Warren Beatty and Faye Dunaway, released

Sweden switches from left to right-hand drive

Che Guevara killed

Christiaan Barnard performs the first heart transplant operation

13 August

5 September

9 October

3 December

The Biafran war and famine brought disturbing images to our screens in 1968. Bringing the stories of death and devastation to viewers almost ended up costing Peter Sissons his life and brought to an end his career as a Foreign Correspondent. He was shot by a Biafran soldier at close range, the bullet passing through both his legs. His cameraman, Cyril Page, tore up his shirt to make a tourniquet to staunch the bleeding and then helped to get Peter to a field dressing station with the aid of an abandoned pram. They made it to a hospital and then to the almost destroyed airport at Lagos where they waited two days for transport out. Peter needed hospital treatment for a year and although the terrible wounds to his legs healed, he was left with a permanent limp. He became a presenter for ITN's *News at One* and *Channel 4 News* before moving to the BBC's *Nine O'Clock News* and *Question Time*.

Above: US troops during an assault on the Vietcong near the Tan Son Nhut Airbase.

Sandy Gall, another foreign correspondent who later became a newscaster, was reporting on the Vietnam war. He was close to the front line in the battle of Hue during the Tet Offensive in Vietnam, a turning point in the war. During the New Year's holiday, or *Tet*, Viet Cong troops and soldiers of the North Vietnamese Army launched a massive assault on the South of the country, taking the American Embassy in Saigon and occupying the ancient capital of Hue. It took American troops four weeks to dislodge them and the vicious, close-quarters fighting left 142 Americans dead.

Tet Offensive begins in Vietnam

The Beatles travel to India to study with the Maharishi Mahesh Yogi

My Lai Massacre in Vietnam

30 January

16 February

16 March

Far left & left: The American public thought they were winning the war, so it was quite a shock when the North Vietnamese Army and the Viet Cong launched the Tet offensive, attacking nearly every major city in South Vietnam. Although they were eventually driven back again, the offensive marked a turning point in public opinion, as many Americans came to believe that their government was misleading them about a war that had no clear end.

Soviet tanks rolled into Czechoslovakia to crush what became known as the 'Prague Spring' – which brought a classic David and Goliath battle onto British television screens. The country's communist leader, Alexander Dubcek, had begun introducing reforms and the people wanted more. One piece of film, broadcast by ITN, was shot by Czech cameramen and smuggled out of the country. One of the cameramen dropped the film – wrapped in brown paper – into a tourist's car near the border with Austria with a note asking that the film be broadcast around the world. It showed an elderly woman screaming defiance at the passing Soviet tanks and the bodies of Czechs, lying in an alley.

Six months after *News at Ten* began, the programme's first 'signoffs' were introduced. The reporter would state their name, the programme and the location. The plan had been to introduce it on a night when there were lots of foreign reports in the programme. All the signoffs had been added but, as fate would have it, a domestic story rose to the top of the running order. The first signoff was, 'Richard Dixon, *News at Ten*, at the Ford works in Dagenham.'

Above: Carnaby Street, centre of Swinging London. Military uniforms were all the rage for the well-dressed dandy about town.

Demonstrations in London against the Vietnam War

Russian cosmonaut Yuri Gagarin is killed on a training flight

Martin Luther King assassinated

2001 – A Space Odyssey is released

17 March

27 March

4 April

6 April

67

Right: Anti-Vietnam War demonstration in London, in March 1968. Protestors – including a young Tariq Ali, marched down Fleet Street and Whitehall. Although it started peacefully, the event descended into violence between police and demonstrators after a fire bomb was let off outside Parliament.

Above: Senator Robert Kennedy's coffin lying in state in St Patrick's Cathedral in New York.

In both the United States and Europe, protests against the Vietnam War grew increasingly angry and violent. ITN's footage of the riots in Grosvenor Square, London, in front of the American Embassy, showed how protesters were using the power of television images to make their point.

The power of moving pictures was also highlighted by Peter Snow's haunting reports on the plight of the starving children of Biafra.

On June 5th, Senator Robert Kennedy – brother of the late President – was himself assassinated as he was about to give a press conference at the Ambassador Hotel in Los Angeles. He was shot with an automatic pistol, at point-blank range, by a Palestinian called Sirhan Sirhan. A few months later, on October 20th, Jackie Kennedy, JFK's widow, married Greek shipping magnate Aristotle Onassis, the richest man in the world.

The Beatles went to visit their guru, the Maharishi Mahesh Yogi, in India. If they were hoping for seclusion and serenity they received anything but. Half the world's cameras – ITN's included – were there. They weren't the only celebrities on the move. Twiggy – a very thin English model – went to Hamburg. Liberace – a very flamboyant American pianist – visited London.

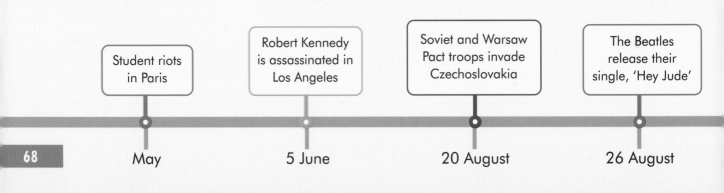

Student riots in Paris	Robert Kennedy is assassinated in Los Angeles	Soviet and Warsaw Pact troops invade Czechoslovakia	The Beatles release their single, 'Hey Jude'
May	5 June	20 August	26 August

Far left: John Lennon walking in the grounds of the Himalayan retreat of the Maharishi Mahesh Yogi. All four Beatles had made the trip at the beginning of 1968, but John and George stayed on after the others had left.

Left: The Maharishi Mahesh Yogi himself. He introduced The Beatles and their entourage to transcendental meditation after they attended a lecture he gave in London the previous year.

In July, *News at Ten* celebrated its first birthday by occupying three of the top four places in the television charts that week. The programme on 1 July – which carried an interview with round the world yachtsman Alec Rose – was number one.

Above: Twiggy, at the height of her fame as a model, attends a fashion show in Hamburg.

Above: American pianist Liberace goes shopping in Carnaby Street during a visit to London. At the time he was featured in the press as the 'Housewives' Heartthrob'...

Above: Liberace considers some Union Jack T-shirts. Good taste prevailed, and he refrained from buying one.

Tommie Smith and John Carlos give the Black Power salute at the Mexico Olympics after winning the Gold and Bronze medals

Jacqueline Kennedy marries Aristotle Onassis

USA spacecraft *Apollo 8* achieves the first manned flight round the moon

16 October

20 October

24 December

1969 Moon Landing

Above: Apollo XI on the launch pad at Cape Kennedy, with its Saturn V rocket ready to lift three astronauts into history.

Above: Lift Off!! The spacecraft lifts off at the start of its long journey to the moon.

Man's greatest challenge proved to be ITN's biggest too. There had been no story like it before – and ITN led the way in how it should be covered.

On Wednesday July16th, *Apollo X1*, powered by a Saturn V rocket, lifted off from the Kennedy Space Center in Florida. Four days later the Apollo astronauts reached the moon. The lunar module, *Eagle*, touched down with Neil Armstrong and Edwin 'Buzz' Aldrin aboard. The third member of the mission team, Michael Collins, remained aboard the command module *Columbia*. A message was relayed back to Mission Control, 'Houston, Tranquillity Base here, the Eagle has landed'. A camera mounted on the lunar module captured the moment that Neil Armstrong descended the ladder and stepped off with his left foot, uttering one of the most famous lines in modern history.

"That's one small step for a man, one giant leap for mankind."

ITN had recognised the magnitude of the event and prepared accordingly. But some in the ITV hierachy took a little convincing. The landing was scheduled to take place at 4am British time and the plan was to carry live coverage all through the night, from 6pm on the preceding evening. The cancellation of an entire Sunday night's schedule, even for an event as momentous as a man on the moon, was a very tough decision. But Sir Lew Grade, head of ATV, sealed the deal when he saw the presentation that ITN had prepared. Having just come from a committee meeting concerned with religious broadcasting, he announced that the moon landing was 'the biggest story since the birth of Christ'!

In the days preceding the launch, ITN's science editor, Peter Fairley gamely donned a space suit in front of a mock-up of the lunar module in order to explain what viewers could expect to see when the big moment came.

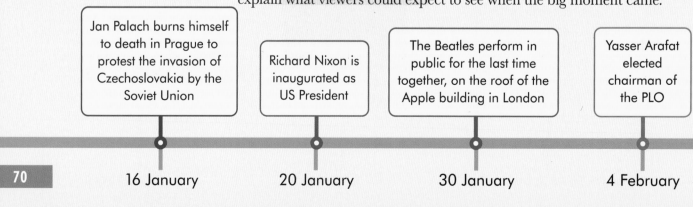

Jan Palach burns himself to death in Prague to protest the invasion of Czechoslovakia by the Soviet Union

Richard Nixon is inaugurated as US President

The Beatles perform in public for the last time together, on the roof of the Apple building in London

Yasser Arafat elected chairman of the PLO

16 January   20 January   30 January   4 February

When it did, ITN's coverage of the moon landing was a triumph and got higher ratings than the BBC – 14.5 million to 12 million. The *Daily Telegraph* reviewed the coverage as 'TV's most exciting show of all time'. Following the unfolding drama live led to an incredible level of suspense. No one knew what would happen, the mission could have ended in catastrophe. As the moment of touchdown approached, the tension became almost unbearable. ITN had devised a plan to explain the complicated codewords the astronauts used. For example '1202, do you copy?' meant 'Shall we abort the mission?' As the *Eagle* descended, the captions explained each staccato exchange. The caption generator, though, was overheating. Just as the legs of the *Eagle* capsule touched the surface of the moon, the final button in the sequence of captions was pressed. The machine then produced the word 'Ouchdown' to describe the greatest moment in space history.

At 4am, after 10 hours of continuous coverage, three and a half million people were still watching, or had got up to watch, and were rewarded with some of the most dramatic images ever to appear on a television screen. When ITN finally went off the air at 6.20 on Monday morning, it had delivered its longest continuous broadcast and won many new admirers.

Above left: Neil Armstrong and Edwin 'Buzz' Aldrin plant the US flag on the surface of the moon.

Above middle: A close view of the lunar landscape, which was pitted with craters and scattered with stones and rocks

Above right: Despite the fact that it was now populated, the moon still looked strangely tranquil...

Above: Edwin 'Buzz' Aldrin, the second man to set foot on the moon.

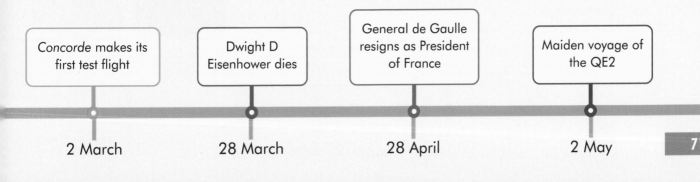

Concorde makes its first test flight

Dwight D Eisenhower dies

General de Gaulle resigns as President of France

Maiden voyage of the QE2

2 March

28 March

28 April

2 May

Above: Queen Elizabeth II travels in the Irish State Coach from Buckingham Palace to the Palace of Westminster, to open Parliament in 1969.

It was a year of colour in more senses than one. As well as reporting the traditional ceremonies of Trooping the Colour and the State Opening of Parliament, ITN's coverage of the investiture of Prince Charles as Prince of Wales was a ratings winner. At the ceremony, held at Caernarfon Castle in Wales, Prince Charles knelt before Queen Elizabeth II to receive the symbols of his new role, before being formally presented to the people of Wales. The BBC's grip on royal events had been prised open.

Such colourful programmes were only now becoming possible as ITN brought in colour cameras. New studios were needed to cope with the new equipment and ITN moved its headquarters from Kingsway to Wells Street in the west end of London. Two new studios were built on the ground floor and there was also plenty of office space as, by now, the number of staff had risen to just over 300.

Right: The ceremony of Trooping the Colour takes place each year in June, to mark the official birthday of Queen Elizabeth II. It is the Queen's Colour of a Foot Guard battalion that is 'trooped' (carried along the ranks) and the five Regiments – Grenadier, Coldstream, Scots, Irish and Welsh – take their turn year by year. The ceremony is a colourful spectacle for tourists, but the soldiers who take part are fully-trained, operational troops.

Midnight Cowboy, starring Dustin Hoffman and Jon Voight, is released

Georges Pompidou elected President of France

Judy Garland dies

Prince Charles invested as Prince of Wales

25 May

20 June

22 June

1 July

Peter Sissons

Peter Sissons was born in Liverpool in 1942. He attended the Liverpool Institute High School and went on to read Modern Greats at University College, Oxford. He joined ITN in 1964 and became a reporter in 1967. While covering the Biafran war in 1968, Sissons was shot through the legs and it is probably only due to the first aid efforts of his cameraman, Cyril Page, that he survived. After a year of hospital treatment he returned to duty and was appointed news editor in 1968. He became industrial correspondent in 1969 and industrial editor in 1972. He moved to *News at One* as an anchorman in 1978 and from there to *Channel 4 News* as the main presenter when the channel was launched in 1982. During his time there, *Channel 4 News* received three BAFTA awards and Peter was honoured with the Royal Television Society's Judges Award for his contribution to the programme. In 1989 he moved to the BBC as presenter of *Question Time* and joint presenter of the *Six O'Clock News*. He was moved to the *Nine O'Clock News*, staying with it when it became the *Ten O'Clock News* in October 2000. Peter Sissons is now a presenter for *BBC News 24*.

Top: The investiture of the Prince of Wales. Prince Charles kneels before his mother, Queen Elizabeth II, at Caernarfon Castle as she prepares to present him with the sword of the Prince of Wales.

Middle: Prince Charles is crowned Prince of Wales, before being presented with the sceptre, ring and an ermine cloak.

Bottom: Queen Elizabeth II presents her eldest son to the people of Wales as their Prince.

Edward M Kennedy crashes his car at Chappaquiddick, killing Mary Jo Kopechne

Apollo XI – The first men on the moon

Woodstock pop festival in upstate New York

British troops are deployed in Northern Ireland

18 July

20 July

August

14 August

1970s

In its early years, television news was considered to be a supplement to the diet of information on events from around the world provided by newspapers and radio. That changed in the 1970s when television became the primary source of news for many people. As television ownership grew, thanks to mass production and the appeal of programmes in colour, television news responded with more up to the moment reporting. The look of television news was changing too with the advent of computer graphics. Cardboard maps and captions were replaced by what then seemed hi-tech images generated by new computer technology.

1970 Conflict

The decade opened with a terrifying event that became a great ITN scoop. Four international airliners were hijacked on the same day – by terrorists belonging to the Popular Front for the Liberation of Palestine – or PFLP.

Below: Palestinian guerrillas from the group Black September and soldiers, next to one of the hijacked planes.

One of the hijackings, led by a woman called Leila Khaled, ended peacefully at Heathrow airport when she was arrested and put in prison in London. Another ended in Cairo. The passengers and crew were allowed off the plane before it was blown up. The pilots of the other two planes were forced to fly to an old RAF airbase, Dawson's Field, in Jordan.

A fifth airliner, a British VC-10, BOAC flight no 775, en route from Bombay to Beirut, was hijacked in reprisal for Leila Khaled's arrest. It too was forced to land at Dawson's Field. The hijackers now held over 300 hostages, 65 of them British, many of them schoolchildren returning from their holidays. The hijackers demanded the release of Khaled, along with other PFLP members, held in

Snowstorms and freezing temperatures across Europe

Biafran forces formally surrender, ending the war for independence from Nigeria

M*A*S*H, starring Donald Sutherland and Elliott Gould, is released

Apollo XIII experiences serious difficulties on the way to the moon, but astronauts finally return safely to earth

January   15 January   February   14 April

Israel, Switzerland and West Germany and they set a three-day deadline. Frantic diplomatic negotiations began, as the hostages endured appalling conditions aboard the grounded airliners.

ITN's Michael Nicholson was dispatched to report on the unfolding drama, accompanied by a Palestinian cameraman, Ghassan Dallal. Then the hijackers announced that the hostages were to be released following the agreement of an exchange deal for Khaled, brokered by Edward Heath's government.

Nicholson and his cameraman witnessed the release of the hostages and then the destruction of the three airliners in a series of massive explosions, which Dallal captured on film. When Nicholson asked him how he knew when to start filming, Dallal replied enigmatically, 'I am a Palestinian'. He was actually a member of the PFLP and took his footage to the PFLP leadership. The ITN team managed to persuade the PFLP leadership to give them back the film, so that the pictures could be shown around the world. The film was flown back to London and made a dramatic start to *News at Ten*. Even the usual headline sequence was dropped – such was the power of the pictures.

Above, left to right: A dramatic series of shots showing the three planes being blown up, one after the other.

The Beatles' LP *Let It Be* is released

Paul McCartney releases his first solo album, *McCartney*

Anti-Vietnam War protests escalate

National Guard opens fire on students at Kent State University in Ohio, USA

17 April

April / May

4 May

8 May

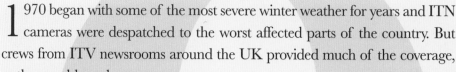

Above: Icy conditions in Holland, in some of the worst winter weather seen for years.

Above: The treacherous icy surface of the road led to many accidents.

1970 began with some of the most severe winter weather for years and ITN cameras were despatched to the worst affected parts of the country. But crews from ITV newsrooms around the UK provided much of the coverage, as they could reach remote areas more easily. A look through the archive catalogue reveals that film and video came from Scottish Television, Grampian, Tyne Tees, Yorkshire and HTV Wales. Covering the weather was just one of very many occasions when ITN was helped by – and even relied on – the news operations of the ITV companies, which is still the case now.

Above: In country areas, some people were trapped by the ice and snow.

With the cold weather came a 'flu epidemic and a rise in the cost of heating oil because of the increased demand.

It wasn't just the UK that was affected by the severe cold though. The big freeze hit other parts of Europe, especially Holland where the icy conditions caused the deaths of large numbers of sea birds.

The Beatles' last album, *Let It Be* was released on Apple Records and protests in song and on the streets against the conflict in Vietnam continued. The war rumbled on, bloodily and hopelessly. And so did the violence in Northern Ireland. It was a dangerous place for journalists and camera crews to operate.

Ted Heath is elected Prime Minister beating Harold Wilson in a surprise result

Aswan High Dam is completed

Palestinians hijack three airliners and blow them up

Jimi Hendrix dies

18 June

21 July

September

18 September

Switching on camera lights drew attention to the crews, but by 1970 there had been an advance in night-time filming. It was called an image intensifier and it used a series of lenses that could be controlled electronically depending on how dark it was, so lights were not necessary so often.

Above: As the Vietnam War dragged on, public opinion began to turn against it.

Martyn Lewis CBE

Martin Lewis was born in Wales but grew up in Northern Ireland. He graduated from Trinity College, Dublin, and joined the BBC in Belfast in 1967. The following year he joined HTV in Cardiff as a reporter and then moved to ITN in 1970 where he became their first North of England correspondent. He returned to London, as a newscaster and foreign correspondent in 1978 and became a presenter on *News at Ten* in 1982. During this time he covered the Falklands War and Pope John Paul II's visit to Britain. In 1986, he left ITN to join the BBC and presented the *One O'Clock News*, the *Six O'Clock News* and the *Nine O'Clock News*, plus *Crimebeat* and *Today's the Day* on BBC2. It was he who announced the death of Princess Diana, having commentated on her wedding to the Prince of Wales whilst with ITN. A prolific author, his books include *Tears and Smiles – The Hospice Handbook*, and *Reflections on Success*, a collection of interviews with prominent personalities including Tony Blair and Stella Rimington. He is involved in much charity work and, in 1997, was awarded the CBE for services to young people and to the hospice movement. He is chairman and co-founder of YouthNet, the first exclusively on-line charity. He is also co-founder of Teleris, acknowledged global leaders in international video conferencing.

Above: In London, a 'flu epidemic led to empty offices and hospitals were overstretched, due to staff shortages and overflowing wards.

Above: A baby elephant gets to know a whole new sensation underfoot.

Richard Nixon begins a tour of Europe, including the United Kingdom

Anwar Sadat becomes president of Egypt

Charles de Gaulle dies

Love Story, starring Ali MacGraw and Ryan O'Neal, is released

27 September

17 October

9 November

16 December

Right: The pyramid stage, made of scaffolding and plastic sheeting, first appeared at Glastonbury in 1971.

Above: A young music-lover waits for the fun to begin. After the '71 festival there was a gap of seven years before the next event, in 1978.

When the ITN newsdesk decided to entrust the coverage of Glastonbury to the ITV company HTV, no one suspected what a phenomenon it was about to become. The first Glastonbury Fayre had been held the previous year and just 1,500 had turned up. In the summer of '71 however, the event had become altogether bigger. The crowds topped 7,000 between June 22nd-26th, over the period of the summer solstice. The story ran and ran. People had come to see Fairport Convention, Joan Baez and David Bowie in what has become revered as one of the most mystical and memorable festivals of all time. Andrew

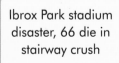

Ibrox Park stadium disaster, 66 die in stairway crush

Idi Amin succeeds Milton Obote in a bloodless coup in Uganda

Rolls Royce goes bankrupt

Earthquake in Los Angeles kills 51

2 January   25 January   4 February   9 February

Left: The fields at Worthy Farm, site of the festival, filled with tents – although considerably less crowded than modern-day events!

Above: Early incarnations of the festival were dominated by hippie ethics and their belief in free music.

Kerr, the festival organiser, had overseen the construction of the pyramid stage, made from steel girders, chicken wire and plastic sheeting and placed over a 'blind spring' – an outlet for cosmic forces generated by the earth itself… At 48 feet high, it was exactly a tenth of the size of the Great Pyramid and was intended to act as a focus for the immense outpouring of psychic energy generated by the festival goers. Kerr even set aside an area on the site as a landing strip for possible flying saucers. As a musical experience, Glastonbury was a success but as a business proposition it failed. The only inhabitants in the fields of Glastonbury for the next few summers were the farmer's cows.

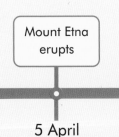

Above: The mud at Glastonbury is almost as famous as the music.

Decimal currency introduced in Britain

British postal strike ends after 47 days

Mount Etna erupts

Bangladesh is created from part of Pakistan

15 February

7 March

5 April

31 May

Above: A cashier learns to operate one of the new decimal tills.

As consumer stories go, they don't get much better than the introduction of decimal currency. ITN's coverage reflected the significance of change in our loose change but also had some fun in the run up to decimalisation and on the day itself in February, asking the public to evaluate the new coins. It was truly a story that affected everyone. Reporter Keith Hatfield went out and about talking to shoppers, train passengers, and market stall holders as they got to grips with the new currency.

Shillings and pennies were replaced by new pence, of which there would be one hundred to the pound. The plan was that, within 18 months, the half-crown, florin, shilling, sixpence, thrupenny bit, penny, and halfpenny would disappear. The Chairman of the Decimal Currency Board, Lord Fiske, was interviewed live on *News at Ten* on Decimalisation Day. He predicted that the changeover would go smoothly and he was just about right. But there was a certain amount of confusion, with price stickers bearing both imperial and decimal figures. There were also accusations of shopkeepers rounding up prices.

Left: Older people found the new coins confusing, although at least the 50p piece had a distinctive shape.

First Glastonbury Festival, following the previous year's Pilton Festival on the same site

June

Norway begins oil production in the North Sea

14 June

Jim Morrison dies

3 July

Violence escalates in Northern Ireland

August

The end of the shilling, then, and almost the end for Rolls Royce in the same month – the company was declared bankrupt. The car company had been founded in 1906, in Manchester, by Charles Stewart Rolls and Frederick Henry Royce, and their first aircraft engine had been produced in 1914. Bentley was absorbed into the company in 1931. The Rolls Royce gained the reputation of being the best car in the world but troubles with the RB 211 aero engine, and poor development plans in the car division helped cause the bankruptcy. It remained, though, the vehicle of choice for rock stars and royalty.

In an unusual move for a Conservative prime minister, Edward Heath nationalised the company and split the aero engine division from the car makers to create Rolls Royce Motors. ITN covered every angle, with reports from the factory gates in Derby, the Stock Exchange and the Houses of Parliament.

One royal making a name for herself, as a sportswoman, was Princess Anne. She not only won the European Three Day Event Trails at Burghley, but was voted Sportswoman of the Year by the Sports Writer's Association and Sports Personality of the Year by the public.

Above: The famous front end of Rolls Royce headed straight into disaster in 1971.

Above: The Royal family turned out in force to watch Princess Anne win the European Horse Trial Championships.

Walt Disney World opens in Florida

John Lennon's LP *Imagine* is released in the UK

A bomb explodes at the top of the Post Office Tower in London

A *Clockwork Orange*, starring Malcolm McDowell and Patrick Magee, is released

1 October

8 October

31 October

19 December

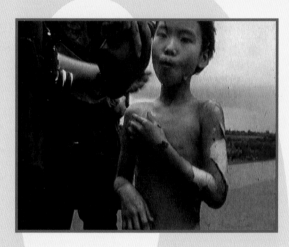

Above left & right: The enduring image of Kim Phuc running from a napalm attack on her village. Her plight did much to convince the public that the Vietnamese War should come to an end.

Of all the shocking images of the shocking war that was Vietnam, the one that endures, that haunts, is that of nine-year-old Kim Phuc, naked, terrified and with her skin peeling off. She was running from a napalm attack on her village, Trang Bang, on June 8th, 1972. The iconic images were filmed by ITN cameraman Alan Downes. A still photograph of the moment, taken by Nick Ut, who subsequently escorted Kim to a hospital, won a Pulitzer Prize.

Kim survived, despite suffering third degree burns to over 50 per cent of her body. She eventually travelled to Cuba to continue her medical studies whilst escaping media attention as a symbol of the war. Ostensibly going on honeymoon with her new, Cuban husband, she defected to Canada during a refuelling stop in Newfoundland, in 1992.

Though the war was to continue for another three years, it was the undeniable power of television pictures that turned American public opinion against it.

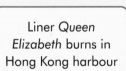

Liner *Queen Elizabeth* burns in Hong Kong harbour

Britain and Eire join the EEC, along with Denmark and Norway

Bloody Sunday – the British Army kills 13 unarmed civil rights marchers

9 January

22 January

30 January

Vietnam has been described as the first television war. Politicians in Washington were eventually forced to order home their troops because of the reaction to nightly pictures of young Americans fighting and dying in Vietnam.

1972 was a frightening year for thousands of Ugandan Asians thrown out by the country's brutal president, Idi Amin, and for reporter Sandy Gall who almost lost his life in one of Amin's jails. First, the President expelled all those who were British passport holders – nearly 50,000 people. Later, he ordered out all Asians, even if they were Ugandan citizens. Sandy was sent to cover the story. While in Uganda, he was taken from his hotel to a military barracks, where he was beaten and thrown into a hut, which was marked C-19. There were bullet holes in the walls and splashes of blood on the ceiling. He was let out to help carry a wounded man to another cell and was eventually allowed to leave the barracks. It was only later Sandy discovered that C-19 was the execution room.

Above: After General Idi Amin took over Uganda he expelled nearly 50,000 thousand British passport holders.

The Olympics in Munich that year should have been memorable for the gymnastics of the Soviet Union's Olga Korbut and the seven gold medals of American swimmer Mark Spitz. But the games will also be remembered for the attack by Palestinian terrorists in which 11 Israeli athletes were killed. The terrorist gang called itself Black September, in memory of the expulsion of the PLO from Jordan in September 1970. Having murdered the Israeli wrestling coach, Moshe Weinberg, the terrorists negotiated an arrangement with West German Chancellor Willi Brandt whereby they would be flown by helicopter to a military airfield, with their 10 hostages, and then transferred to a flight to an Arab country. At the Furstenfeld military airfield, the police fired on the terrorists as they crossed the tarmac to their waiting plane. In the ensuing fire fight, all of the hostages and four of the eight terrorists died. One of the remaining terrorists managed to escape and the three who were captured were released within weeks when Black September hijacked a Lufthansa airliner.

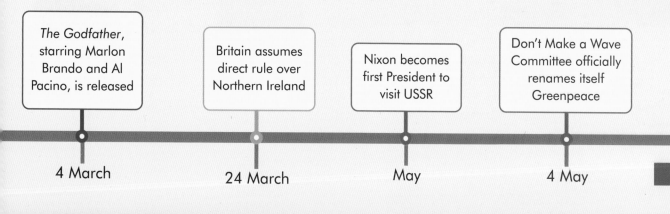

The Godfather, starring Marlon Brando and Al Pacino, is released

Britain assumes direct rule over Northern Ireland

Nixon becomes first President to visit USSR

Don't Make a Wave Committee officially renames itself Greenpeace

4 March

24 March

May

4 May

Below: On Bloody Sunday – January 30th 1972 – a civil rights march in Northern Ireland turned into a massacre when British soldiers opened fire: 13 marchers were killed. Rioting followed, with many protestors throwing petrol bombs before being arrested.

By the seventies, the Northern Ireland troubles were an all too regular part of ITN programmes and there was a permanent ITN presence there. Reporter Gerald Seymour knew the patch and was assigned to cover a civil rights march in Londonderry. He knew it was going to be a big story and asked for an extra camera crew, but even he was not prepared for what happened that day – Sunday January 30th. 13 people were shot dead by soldiers of the Parachute Regiment and, not surprisingly, it became known as Bloody Sunday.

The march had progressed peacefully but as the demonstrators gathered to listen to an address by their leaders, a gang of perhaps 100 youngsters began to hurl stones and abuse at the British troops who were policing the event. The soldiers responded with tear gas and baton rounds and then, believing that they were being fired on, with live ammunition. A series of IRA 'reprisals' followed including the bombing of the Parachute Regiment's headquarters in Aldershot a month later.

What happened that day has been the subject of two major inquiries. The most recent, conducted by Lord Saville, began in 1998, and lasted seven years. His report is due in 2006.

Little more than a week before Bloody Sunday, Prime Minister Edward Heath had signed the Treaty of Brussels, the document that would make Britain a member of the European Economic Community the following year. This was regarded by many as his greatest triumph and by others as a betrayal. ITN carried pictures of the anti-European demonstrations in

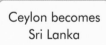

Ceylon becomes Sri Lanka

Japanese terrorists kill 25 Israelis at Lod Airport, Tel Aviv

Idi Amin announces the expulsion of Ugandan Asians

Iceland extends its fishing limit to 50 miles – The Cod War

22 May

30 May

August

August

London. Its pictures of the signing were provided by the European Broadcasting Union, in what is known as a pool arrangement. At major news events, competing news companies agree to a single crew filming the proceedings then sharing the pictures – this avoids too many cameras being packed into a news conference in a small, crowded or historic location such as Egmont Palace in Brussels.

Above: A British soldier patrols the streets of Londonderry as the violence dies down.

Leonard Parkin

Leonard Parkin was born in 1931, in Yorkshire. He worked there as a journalist until joining the BBC as a television news reporter in 1954. From 1963 to 1965 he was the BBC's Washington correspondent and then worked as a reporter on *Panorama*. In 1967 he moved to ITN and was part of the founding team of *News at Ten* newsreaders. He presented *News at 5.45* from 1975 to 1978 and then moved to *News at One*. He reported for ITN from India and the Middle East and covered the US elections in 1972 and the French elections in 1980. Leonard Parkin retired from ITN in 1987 but continued to make documentaries, returning to his roots in Yorkshire to make *Slices of Parkin*. He died in 1993, following a long battle with cancer.

Above: Edward Heath signs Great Britain up to the EEC.

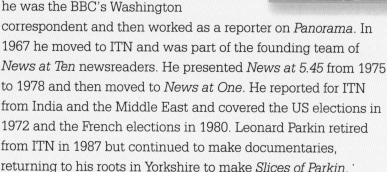

Mark Spitz wins seven gold medals at the Munich Olympics

Break-in at the Democratic Party HQ in the Watergate Building

Bloody Friday – 22 bombs explode in Belfast, nine people are killed and 130 seriously injured

11 athletes are killed after members of the PLO organisation Black September storm the Israeli compound and take hostages

August   17 June   21 June   5 September

Above left to right: The spring shows in Paris reveal what the well-dressed woman will be wearing that year. The full length, patterned dresses were hailed as a return to the 'body beautiful' style.

The Paris fashions brought plenty of glamour and colour to ITN programmes in 1973. Reporter Victoria Brittain was sent to cover the unveiling of that year's spring and summer collections. ITN broadcast three reports in a week from the *Salons*.

One of the main themes was the Asian influence over European fashion. Japan's Issey Miyake was showing his collection in Paris for the first time – following in the footsteps of Takada Kenzo. The Japanese used the traditions of their culture: boldness and purity of line and melding of colour and textures.

Yom Kippur War begins when Egyptian and Syrian forces attack Israel

General Pinochet seizes power in Chile

Arab states cut oil supplies to the West

11 September

October

6 October

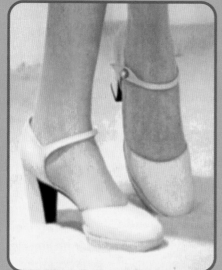

A certain Trevor McDonald, a 33-year-old Trinidadian, joined ITN as a general reporter. The *Daily Telegraph* covered the announcement like this: 'The snappy presentation of Independent Television News will be strengthened by the arrival of their first black reporter. Trevor McDonald is at present an interviewer on the BBC's *World Service*. "I am not at all nervous about changing from radio to television," he says. "I think I'll be able to produce a different outlook on the news."'

Above: Trevor Macdonald first joined ITN in 1973.

Britain issues petrol coupons

Princess Anne marries Captain Mark Phillips

Nixon protests his innocence in the Watergate affair to a conference of journalists

Three Day Week – Britain declares a State of Emergency

November

14 November

17 November

31 December

Above: Prince Charles begins helicopter flying lessons during his stint with the Royal Navy.

ITN stole a march on the BBC in its reporting of the attempted shooting of Princess Anne on March 20th. A car had blocked the path of the Princess's chauffeur-driven Rolls Royce in Pall Mall as she and her husband, Captain Mark Phillips were returning to Buckingham Palace after an official engagement. A man called Ian Ball fired a number of shots from a hand gun, injuring by-standers, before himself being wounded by a shot fired by the Princess's private detective. He attempted to run off but was apprehended by a policeman. It was reported that, when Ball informed the Princess, at gunpoint, that he intended to kidnap her, she replied 'Not bloody likely!'

Because there was a commercial break at 8.46pm on ITV that night, ITN was able to break the news within a couple of minutes of it coming through. The BBC waited until 9pm. But ITN's advantage didn't stop there. *News at Ten* had the scoop of an eyewitness who not only saw what happened but actually spoke to Princess Anne. Sammy Scott described how frightening it had been when Ball began shaking the doors of the car with just the Princess and Captain trapped inside. When Ball ran off, Miss

Above left: Princess Anne was the subject of an attempted kidnap in Pall Mall when returning from an official engagement.

Above right: The Princess was also enjoying success in her riding career.

The General Election produces a hung parliament, but finally Harold Wilson becomes Prime Minister

Princess Anne escapes a kidnap attempt in The Mall

BEA merges with BOAC to form British Airways

28 February

20 March

31 March

Scott got inside the car and asked the Princess 'Are you all right, love?' and received the reply, 'Yes, I'm fine thank you.' Ball was discovered to be mentally unstable and committed to an institution where he remains to this day, protesting his innocence.

There was rather happier news for the Princess's big brother that year. Prince Charles was beginning helicopter flying lessons while serving with the Royal Navy and making a good job of it – in front of the world's media. His instructor described the Prince as 'a natural pilot'. His course at the Yeovilton naval base in Somerset lasted three and a half months. He'd already qualified as a jet pilot while serving with the RAF.

1974 was the year of two General Elections. The Conservative Government of Prime Minister Edward Heath had been crippled by the miners' strike and the oil crisis. He called an election to try and get a mandate from the country but failed by the narrowest of margins. Labour's Harold Wilson formed the next Government and then called a second election in October to try and get an overall majority.

Above: Prime Minister Harold Wilson, with his wife, Mary.

ITN produced election results programmes for both. Television graphics in the early seventies relied on pieces of card with Letraset captions, placed in front of a camera. After the February election, ITN bosses decided there had to be a better way... an electronic way. Computers were pretty unsophisticated but they hit on the idea of adapting a machine used to show what Fair Isle knitting patterns would look like when they were made up. By the October election, ITN had a computer called VT30. It could show not knitting patterns, but it was possible to see electoral patterns emerging during the course of election night.

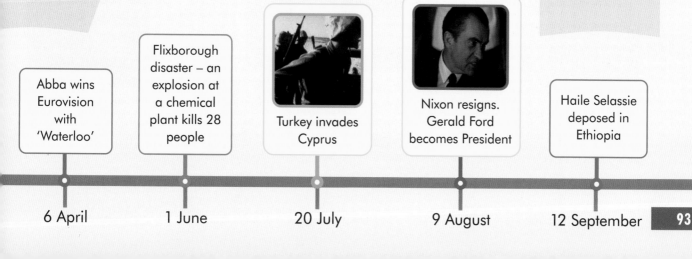

Abba wins Eurovision with 'Waterloo'

Flixborough disaster – an explosion at a chemical plant kills 28 people

Turkey invades Cyprus

Nixon resigns. Gerald Ford becomes President

Haile Selassie deposed in Ethiopia

6 April   1 June   20 July   9 August   12 September

Below: Families flee their homes, carrying a few possessions, as Turkey invades Cyprus.

The Flixborough chemical factory disaster killed 28 people and at first no one was sure what had caused it, until an ITN exclusive revealed the true situation.

As the ITN team flew in by helicopter, they could see, from 50 miles away, a bright orange glow in the sky. The factory, near Scunthorpe, was totally destroyed by explosions and fire. Reporter Keith Hatfield filed his story for that evening's bulletins but he didn't stop there. He wanted to find someone from the factory to interview. When all the other reporters had left the scene the works manager finally turned up looking, not surprisingly, shattered. He told Keith he thought that a faulty join in a repair on a broken pipe was to blame, by causing a build up of explosive vapour. Keith included the information in his reports the following day. A year later, the inquiry into the disaster confirmed the suspicions of the works manager.

There was another big ITN exclusive during the Turkish invasion of Cyprus. Turkish troops had been expected to land on the coast – providing the pictures that the world's news organisations had been waiting for. ITN reporter Michael Nicholson was in Cyprus to cover the story when he received a tip-off from colleague Peter Snow back in London that something was about to happen. Michael and his crew set off for the coast – expecting to see amphibious landings. As luck would have it, their rented car ran out of petrol. The BBC crew drove past them and it looked like ITN was going to miss the story. Then Michael and his team heard the drone of aircraft above them. A passing student who knew all about ITN from time spent in the UK offered to give them a lift and took them to what

'Rumble in the Jungle' – Ali regains his World Heavyweight boxing title, fighting George Foreman in Zaire

Birmingham bombings in two pubs, killing 21 people

Guildford Pub bombings by the IRA

5 October

30 October

21 November

became the drop zone for hundreds of Turkish paratroopers. Michael was able to greet some of them with a handshake as they landed and with the words, 'I'm Michael Nicholson of ITN. Welcome to Cyprus!'

Above: Michael Nicholson, reporting the invasion as it happened.

Michael Nicholson

• • • • • • • • • • • • • • • •

Michael Nicholson joined ITN in 1964. He was interviewed by Geoffrey Cox, who thought that he had been working for the publishers of *The Sunday Times*, Thomson Newspapers, when in fact he was employed by D. C. Thomson, who published *The Beano*. Nonetheless, he started work in the newsroom. Starting with a report on an injured robber escaping from hospital, in South London, Nicholson went on to provide ITN with some of their most dramatic reports and biggest scoops. It was Michael Nicholson who managed to interview Turkish paratroopers as they landed on Cyprus; who covered the Yom Kippur War of 1973, reporting from the Golan Heights, and was forced to fight his way into the American Embassy compound to escape during the chaos of the fall of Saigon in 1975. Michael Winterbottom's film *Welcome to Sarajevo* was based on Nicholson's efforts to evacuate children during the Balkan Conflict of 1992.

In 1999 he left ITN to join Granada TV as a correspondent for their *Tonight* programme. Among his many successes in his new role was his on the spot reporting of the toppling of Saddam Hussein's statue in Baghdad, at the end of the second Gulf War in 2003.

Above: Turkish paratroopers land and plant the Turkish flag on Cyprus.

Paul McCartney and Wings release the LP, *Band on the Run*

The Towering Inferno, starring Steve McQueen and Paul Newman, is released

Lord Lucan disappears

Darwin, Australia, is almost completely destroyed by Cyclone Tracy

30 November

10 December

12 December

24 December

Above: A Marine helicopter lands on the US Embassy roof in Saigon, ready to evacuate staff and as many others as possible.

Above middle: People crowd around the Embassy swimming pool, hoping to get onto one of the evacuation flights.

Above right: More hopeful evacuees sit round on the Embassy roof.

The world's first television war, the conflict in Vietnam, finally ended with appropriately dramatic pictures of the withdrawal of US diplomats and troops from the roof of the American Embassy in the capital, Saigon. ITN's Michael Nicholson and his camera crew were among those who had to scramble and fight their way onto one of the relay of American helicopters, amid scenes of utter chaos and confusion.

Nicholson described the ignominy of the departure in a memorable report from an American warship in the South China Sea. He reported how he and his crew had had to claw their way over the gates of the embassy. They only made it thanks to one US marine who hauled them up, kicking and punching South Vietnamese civilians who were desperate to get into the compound to escape the North Vietnamese troops.

When the platoon of US Marines who had protected the evacuees finally clambered aboard the last helicopter, the Vietnam war was finally at an end. It had lasted for nearly two decades, cost the lives of nearly 60,000 Americans

Margaret Thatcher defeats Ted Heath to become leader of the Conservatives

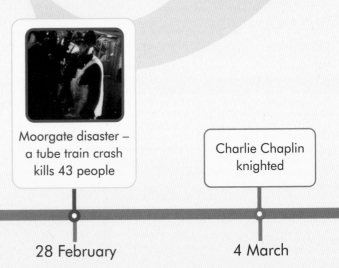

Moorgate disaster – a tube train crash kills 43 people

Charlie Chaplin knighted

11 February

28 February

4 March

and probably somewhere in the region of a million Vietnamese troops and four million civilians. Many soldiers from Australia and New Zealand had also died in the conflict.

Sandy Gall had been covering the end of the war and he agreed to stay when it was learned a BBC crew had decided to remain in Saigon. Sandy and a French camera crew he was working with secured remarkable footage of the arrival of the victorious North Vietnamese Army, but there was no way of getting the film out of the country. The North Vietnamese had cut all the phone and telex links so there wasn't even any way of telling ITN what was going on. Sandy managed to persuade the victorious North Vietnamese general that the only way the world would see his triumphal arrival was if he lent Sandy a plane. A fortnight later, Sandy managed to get out – but in the end he need not have rushed. The ITV network was on strike over a new national pay deal and Sandy's remarkable report was finally broadcast a month after the fall of Saigon.

The first handshake in space between American astronauts and Soviet cosmonauts was scheduled for July 17th. ITN's space consultant, Geoff Perry, had worked out that once the *Apollo* and *Soyuz* spacecrafts joined up, the handshake would take place high above Bognor Regis in West Sussex. NASA confirmed the calculation and the newspaper headlines in Britain read, 'Bognor, here we come!' But it wasn't to be. The cosmonauts waited for the astronauts to make the first move and the delay meant the handshake happened as the docked spacecraft drifted over Northern France.

Above: In another remote part of the world, Shetland Islanders were fighting to retain their links with the mainland.

Above: Meanwhile, Covent Garden held the first Festival of Real Ale.

US Embassy in Saigon is evacuated, and Saigon is taken by Communist forces, ending the Vietnam War

Britain votes yes in the referendum on staying in the EEC

Jaws, starring Roy Scheider, Robert Shaw and Richard Dreyfuss, is released

US and Soviet spacecraft dock in space and the two commanders shake hands

30 April

June

20 June

17 July

Above: Fireman at Moorgate after the tube crash that killed 43 people.

For five days at the end of February and the beginning of March, ITN programmes were dominated by the crash of a tube train at Moorgate on the London Underground. 43 people died when the train slammed into a blocked-off tunnel, hitting a brick wall at 30 miles per hour. The exact cause of the accident has never been ascertained. There were no faults with either the train or the track and the driver was experienced and had been in good health. It happened in the morning rush hour but it wasn't until late evening that the last of the survivors was pulled out. It took five days to get all the bodies out.

Part of ITN's coverage centred on the injuries to new WPC Margaret Liles who had only been in the job for a week. She was a passenger in the first carriage and had to have part of her leg amputated to be cut free, but she did survive.

Above and above right: Silent streets outside the Spaghetti House restaurant in Knightsbridge, as police negotiate for the release of hostages.

British Leyland is taken over by the government	Haile Selassie dies	Spaghetti House restaurant siege in London	Prince Juan Carlos becomes King of Spain, since Franco is in poor health
11 August	27 August	September / October	30 October

In another dark episode in the capital, armed robbers held nine waiters hostage in a Knightsbridge restaurant in what became known as the 'Spaghetti House' siege. The three robbers burst in as the managers of the three restaurants in the chain met to pay in the week's takings. They held nine of the waiters but a tenth escaped to raise the alarm. The police cordoned off the area and the gunmen, claiming to be members of a group that didn't actually exist, demanded to be put on a plane to a neutral destination. After six days the robbers gave themselves up.

There was a second siege in December. IRA gunmen who had murdered Ross McWhirter, co-founder of the *Guinness Book of Records* and a staunch opponent of the Irish Republicans, were pursued through the streets of London by armed police. They took refuge in a flat in Balcombe Street, Marylebone, taking the two residents hostage. After six days, and knowing that SAS had been brought in, the gunmen surrendered.

And finally… Margaret Thatcher beat off four male rivals to succeed Edward Heath as the new leader of the Conservative Party. Mrs Thatcher's assessment of her achievement: 'I beat four chaps. Now let's get down to business'.

Above: The end of the Balcombe Street siege, above left, as one of the IRA gunmen comes out on the balcony, above, to give himself up.

Above: Margaret Thatcher becomes Leader of the Conservative Party.

General Franco dies

Ross McWhirter shot dead by IRA

Balcombe Street siege in London

20 November

27 November

December

1976 Concorde

Below: Concorde was developed by the British Aircraft Corporation and Sud Aviation of France in partnership. Concorde 001 was built in Toulouse, in France.

The age of supersonic commercial flights began in a blaze of publicity, hours of television air time – and a thunderous roar with the first Concorde passenger flights in January. The idea of producing a British supersonic airliner dated back to the end of the Second World War but the project only started taking off in the sixties, with the development of

Above: The distinctive Concorde delta wing shape.

Concorde by the British Aircraft Corporation and Sud Aviation of France. By the beginning of 1976, the aircraft was certified and ready for service. The United States was still unwilling to grant Concorde access to major American destinations – on environmental grounds – but both British Airways and Air France were keen to demonstrate their spectacular new aircraft as quickly as possible. So at 11.40am on January 21st, British and French Concordes took off simultaneously from London and Paris, bound for Bahrain and Rio de Janeiro respectively. Among the privileged passengers were the transport secretaries of both governments and the chief executives of the airlines. Brian Trubshaw, the chief test pilot, was also aboard. Concorde services to America began with flights to Dulles International Airport, Washington DC, in May, and the New York service, which proved to be the aircraft's most popular and lucrative route, started in late 1977. Concorde continued in service until 2003. Its end was hastened by a terrible crash, near Paris in July 2000. Concorde, despite its

Concorde begins commercial flights

The *Olympic Bravery* goes aground off Brittany, spilling 250,000 tons of oil

John Curry wins Britain's first gold medal for figure skating at the Olympics in Innsbruck

21 January

24 January

11 February

Anglo-French heritage, became a symbol of British engineering excellence. It was cramped and noisy but it could fly at more than twice the speed of sound and turned heads skyward wherever it flew.

Above: The British test pilot, Brian Trubshaw, and his French counterpart, Andre Turcat, pose after a test flight of the British-built Concorde 002 at Filton, near Bristol.

Sir Alastair Burnet

● ● ● ● ● ● ● ● ● ● ● ● ● ● ● ●

Alastair Burnet was born in Edinburgh in 1928. He went to school in Cambridge and then to University at Oxford. He first joined ITN in 1963 as political editor but left two years later to become editor of the *The Economist*. This appointment lasted until 1974. It was during this time that he returned to ITN to head the team of newscasters during the three-month trial of *News at Ten*. He left the *Economist* to become editor of the *Daily Express* until 1976 when he moved back permanently to ITN, first as a newscaster on the *News at 5.45* programme and then back to *News at Ten*. He became the authoritative voice of ITN, describing the Apollo space missions, the wedding of Prince Charles and Lady Diana Spencer, the visit to Britain of Pope John Paul II and numerous other major events. He has been presented with the Richard Dimbleby Award on four occasions and was nominated Political Broadcaster of the year in 1979. He is the author of four books on the Royal Family and was knighted in 1984 for his services to journalism and broadcasting.

Above: Concorde comes in to land, with its nose pointing down to improve the pilot's view.

Above: Celebrations at the official debut of Concorde at Toulouse.

Apple computer company is founded by Steve Jobs and Steve Wozniak

Jim Callaghan takes over as Prime Minister after Harold Wilson resigns

Concorde begins a service to Washington DC

24 March

1 April

5 April

Above left: Jimmy Carter becomes President of the United States of America.

Above right: One of President Carter's greatest achievements was the Camp David Agreement between Egypt and Israel.

On the political front there was much to report. Jimmy Carter, a peanut farmer from Plains, Georgia, beat Gerald R. Ford in the Bicentennial US election to be sworn in as the 39th President of the United States the following year. The election had been called following the resignation of President Nixon over the Watergate scandal. During his presidency, Carter strove very hard to contain inflation and to shore up a struggling US economy, and he succeeded as well as any man could. His policies helped to create some eight million jobs and to reduce the budget deficit. One of his greatest achievements was to broker the Camp David agreement of 1978 between Israel and Egypt. He also established full diplomatic relations between the US and China and completed the negotiations for the second Strategic Arms Limitation Treaty with the Soviet Union. The low point of his administration was undoubtedly the debacle of the US Embassy hostage crisis in Iran in 1979.

In Britain, Harold Wilson resigned as Prime Minister. He made the announcement live – which was carried by an ITN outside broadcast unit. He'd told his press secretary, 'Tell the lobby correspondents you've got a little story that might interest them'. He said he would be leaving politics and public life altogether. This came as a complete shock to the nation and to many of those close to him in government. Wilson claimed that it had always been his intention to resign at the age of 60 and that he was mentally and physically exhausted. It may be, however, that he was aware of the fact that

End of the Cod War between UK and Iceland

Israeli troops storm the captured airliner at Entebbe and rescue 94 of the 98 hostages

USA celebrates its bicentennial and Queen Elizabeth II attends the celebrations

1 June

3 July

4 July

his health was deteriorating – he was suffering from early-onset Alzheimer's disease. He was succeeded by Jim Callaghan, who saw off the challenges of Michael Foot, Tony Benn, and Roy Jenkins.

The Cod War between Britain and Iceland was a dramatic story that was proving very difficult to illustrate on television. British trawlers that defied a self-proclaimed 50-mile Icelandic exclusion zone were having their nets cut by Iceland's small fleet of gunboats. Royal Navy frigates were deployed to protect the British fishermen. But any kind of confrontation at sea was sporadic and unpredictable.

Then ITN reporter Norman Rees hit on the idea of trying to get on board one of the Icelandic gunboats. The Icelandic government eventually agreed and after a couple of days on board the *Thor* Norman and his camera crew got the incident they had been waiting for. It was a chase on the high seas, as a Royal Navy frigate, *HMS Leander*, moved in to protect a British trawler from the cutting gear of the *Thor*. It ended with a big collision that left both vessels damaged.

To ITN viewers, it looked like the Navy was acting tough and protecting the British trawlers. But the pictures went down well too in Iceland, when they were shown there. The Icelanders liked seeing their gunboats taking on the mighty Royal Navy and giving it a bloody nose. When Norman and the ITN crew returned to Reykjavik they were given a heroes' welcome – with a brass band and local dignitaries waiting on the quayside.

Above: In Britain, James Callaghan became Prime Minister, after the resignation of Harold Wilson.

Above: In the Cod War, Iceland and Britain finally resolved their differences.

Chinese leader Chairman Mao dies

Rocky, starring Sylvester Stallone, is released

Sex Pistols cause outrage by swearing on ITV's *Today* show

The Eagles release their album *Hotel California*

9 September

21 November

1 December

8 December

Above left: Queen Elizabeth II and the Duke of Edinburgh at a photocall to mark the beginning of the Jubilee celebrations.

Above middle: The Queen travels to St Paul's Cathedral in the State Coach, for a service of thanksgiving.

Above right: The Queen made a speech thanking the people of Britain and the Commonwealth for the celebrations.

As Queen Elizabeth celebrated 25 years on the throne, *News at Ten* celebrated 10 years on the air. The Silver Jubilee captured the imagination of the public. ITN's coverage captured the genuine sense of thanksgiving in the country but also the colour of the informal celebrations – during the year there were almost endless street parties, fêtes and festivities of just about every sort. There was a certain amount of cashing in, as a fizzy drink called Jubilade was launched and there were special jubilee ice creams, beers, cakes, and even margarine. Buses were painted silver, coins were minted, stamps were printed and millions of souvenirs, of varying degrees of tastelessness, were produced and sold to a seemingly insatiable market. The main commemoration was held on June 7th, in London. Both Houses of Parliament delivered loyal addresses. On the eve of Jubilee Day, a chain of beacons was lit across the land and, in the morning, immense crowds turned out to see the Queen drive in the gold State Coach to St Paul's Cathedral for a special service of thanksgiving,

Punk rock group the Sex Pistols are dropped by EMI but later signed by the fledgling Virgin recording company

Jimmy Carter becomes US President

Fleetwood Mac release their album *Rumours*

6 January

20 January

4 February

attended by representatives of many governments and numerous heads of state. It was the first time the coach had been used since the Coronation. Later, at a lunch hosted by the Lord Mayor of London, the Queen said,

'My Lord Mayor, when I was 21 I pledged my life to the service of our people and I asked for God's help to make good that vow. Although that vow was made in my salad days, when I was green in judgment, I do not regret nor retract one word of it'.

When the lunch ended, the Queen did a walkabout through the City of London. A small boy who approached her with an autograph book was told by an equerry, 'The Queen only signs Acts of Parliament'. The little boy had to settle for a chat with Prince Philip instead. Around the world an estimated half a billion people watched as the Queen returned to Buckingham Palace and appeared on the balcony to the delight of the tens of thousands of well-wishers who had crowded into the Mall and turned it into a sea of red, white and blue.

Above: On Jubilee Day itself, the Queen did a walkabout and stopped to talk to some of the thousands of people who had turned out to cheer.

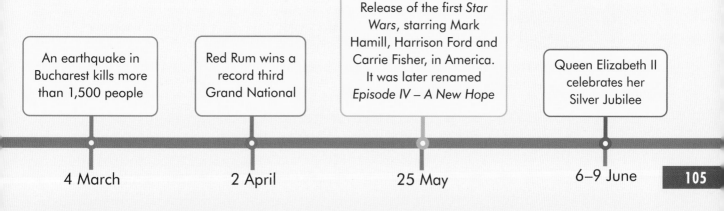

An earthquake in Bucharest kills more than 1,500 people

Red Rum wins a record third Grand National

Release of the first *Star Wars*, starring Mark Hamill, Harrison Ford and Carrie Fisher, in America. It was later renamed *Episode IV – A New Hope*

Queen Elizabeth II celebrates her Silver Jubilee

4 March

2 April

25 May

6–9 June

Above: A young Elvis goes off to Germany in his service days.

Far right: His army experiences were put to good use in his 1960 film *G.I. Blues*.

The news of the death of Elvis Presley on August 16th caused a few moments of uncertainty among the *News at Ten* team. Four minutes before the programme was about to end, a one line 'snap' came through from the Associated Press news agency on the teleprinters. Reginald Bosanquet announced that reports of the singer's death were coming in. A minute or so later another one line report came up on the same agency saying Elvis had been taken to hospital. That seemed to raise the possibility that perhaps he wasn't dead after all. *News at Ten* ended with Reggie saying... 'and Elvis Presley is dead – or is he?'

Straight after the programme the ITN foreign desk checked with Associated Press who were able to explain. They had issued the report about Elvis being taken to hospital first. When they heard he had died they released a second report and 'flashed' or prioritised it, so it was sent out before the first one. Reggie went back on the air at the next break to clear up the confusion and to confirm the sad news that Elvis had died, apparently of heart failure. It was only later that rumours of a drugs overdose began to circulate.

Fans from across the United States and across the world converged on Graceland, Presley's Memphis mansion. The distance from Graceland to the cemetery where he was to be buried was only three miles, but on the day of his funeral the journey took his funeral cortège almost an hour. The route was lined by fans who repeatedly broke through the police lines.

Violent clashes between police and strikers in Britain

Manchester United manager Tommy Docherty is sacked by the club's directors

A power blackout in New York City lasts for 25 hours and leads to looting and disorder

July

4 July

13 July

In London, ITN covered a memorial service for Elvis at a church in North London, held two days after his death. More than 1,000 fans took part.

Elvis was born in January 1935, the son of a poor cotton farmer in the southern state of Tennessee. His identical twin brother was stillborn. On his 12th birthday his parents gave him a guitar, beginning one of the greatest show business careers in history… a career that was to earn the singer millions of dollars and make him a household name throughout the world. During his 20 year career, Presley starred in more than 60 films and received 25 'Golden Discs'… awarded for sales of more than one million copies.

Far left: Priscilla and Elvis on their wedding day. Their daughter, Lisa Marie, was staying at Graceland at the time Elvis died, although he and Priscilla had been divorced for some time.

Left and far left: Police and pickets clash during a strike at the Grunwick Processing Laboratory, in July 1977.

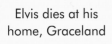

Elvis dies at his home, Graceland

Civil rights leader Steve Biko dies in police custody in South Africa

Freddie Laker launches *Skytrain*

Charlie Chaplin dies

16 August

12 September

26 September

25 December

Above: The stricken *Amoco Cadiz* off the cost of Brittany.

Right: The oil from the tanker washed ashore along both sides of the English Channel.

Above: The effect on wildlife was catastrophic – nearly 20,000 birds were killed, as well as fish and other sea creatures.

The fifth largest oil spill in history hit the Brittany coast of France in March and ITN's John Suchet was sent to cover the story. The super tanker *Amoco Cadiz* had run onto rocks after its rudder broke and the 222,000 tonnes of crude oil that it was carrying made a slick that was, at one stage, 18 miles long and 80 miles wide. John reported the efforts made to contain the oil, which was difficult in the stormy sea, and then the efforts to clean the beaches. But it was the pictures of sea birds trapped in oily water that pulled at the heart strings of the viewers. Around 20,000 birds were killed and countless fish and other sea creatures were washed up on the shore for weeks after the accident. The beaches of 76 different Breton communities were affected by the oil. The authorities tried everything to stop it spreading – at one point a helicopter was brought in to drop depth charges to blow up the wreck when the wind was blowing away from the shore.

Sweden becomes the first nation to ban aerosol sprays in fears about the ozone layer

Rhodesia attacks Zambia

Anna Ford becomes *News at Ten*'s first female presenter

Amoco Cadiz runs aground in Brittany, spilling 220,000 tons of oil

23 January   3 March   9 March   16 March

The ITN team in Brittany had parcelled up some of the oil from the beaches and sent it back to London. In the *News at Ten* studio, Reggie Bosanquet placed it in front of the camera and then discussed the disaster and the ways of dealing with it, with Sir Eric Drake, former Chairman of BP. At one stage Reggie poured some of the oil into a glass of water to show, despite how thick and heavy it appeared, it would always rise to the surface.

However, ITN's greatest drama of the year was kept quiet at the time. Michael Nicholson, along with his cameraman, Tom Phillips, and sound recordist, Micky Doyle, were in Angola, covering the civil war between the South African backed UNITA rebels and Angolan government troops. They were on what they thought was a 10 day trip. It ended up lasting exactly 100 days longer than they had expected.

Shortly after their arrival, the UNITA vehicle in which Nicholson, Phillips and Doyle were travelling was ambushed and destroyed. The ambush coincided with a major offensive being launched by pro-government forces against UNITA and the team was trapped by the fighting. Their only chance of escape lay in trekking with UNITA soldiers back to their base, which lay 1,500 miles away. The journey took seven and a half weeks, marching from dawn till dusk, living on maize porridge and cooked insects. They couldn't travel in straight lines because of the danger of walking into enemy strongholds and had to cope with scorpions, snakes, plagues of flies, intense heat and the physical punishment and mental monotony of marching for up to 12 hours a day. Micky Doyle suffered terribly – his feet became badly ulcerated and he collapsed during the march. ITN was getting increasingly worried about them and, at one stage, had four chartered planes standing by at different locations while attempts were made to make contact with the missing men. By the time they reached the UNITA base, they were emaciated and exhausted. Tom Phillips had lost five stones – but they had survived to tell their remarkable tale.

Above: Workers in protective clothing attempt to clean up the oil on the beach.

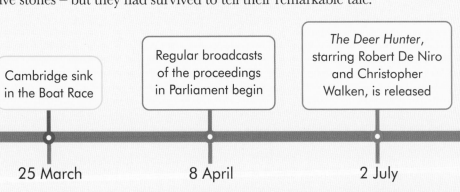

Cambridge sink in the Boat Race

Regular broadcasts of the proceedings in Parliament begin

The Deer Hunter, starring Robert De Niro and Christopher Walken, is released

First test tube baby, Louise Brown, is born

25 March

8 April

2 July

25 July

Above: The Sex Pistols on stage at Atlanta, Georgia.

Anna Ford replaced Andrew Gardner on *News at Ten* and was warmly welcomed by Reggie Bosanquet. They soon established an excellent rapport and became one of the programme's most effective 'double acts'. Andrew was a tough act to follow so Anna was allowed to settle in gradually to the ITN way of doing things. She read some weekend bulletins, did some reporting and presented *News at One*. Her supposed BBC rival Angela Rippon sent her a telegram of congratulations saying 'Well done, welcome to the club'. On the night Anna officially joined *News at Ten* Reggie placed a bottle of red wine and two glasses on her desk. It was at this time that one of the most celebrated 'And, finally…' stories occurred. It concerned a cat, stuck up a tree. The elderly lady owner had summoned the fire brigade to rescue it, but there was a firemen's strike and the army were standing in with their 'Green Goddess' fire engines. The soldiers duly arrived and gallantly obliged. The old lady repaid them with tea and biscuits. Tragedy struck, however, when the squad drove off and ran over the cat. Unfortunately, Reggie couldn't stop himself chuckling at the irony of it all and ITN's switchboard was jammed by calls from outraged cat lovers.

In the music world the Sex Pistols were busy being bad. Their rendition of 'God Save The Queen' in the Jubilee year had caused considerable consternation and generated considerable sales. Their infamous altercation with Bill Grundy on Thames Television's early evening *Today* programme, during which the 'F' word was uttered, more than once, had already passed into legend. They now embarked on a tour of the United States, where their reception was… mixed. ITN caught up with some of the pierced American teenagers who'd turned out to see the band. One of the fans told ITN, 'They were great. If only I could make out the words, they would be even greater'.

Bar codes were introduced on groceries – a novelty then although on everything now. Muhammad Ali was defeated by Leon Spinks in Las Vegas, Nevada, but regained his World Heavyweight Champion's title

Pope Paul VI dies

Turin Shroud displayed for the first time in 45 years

Israel and Egypt reach agreement at Camp David

Newspaper boy Carl Bridgwater is shot dead after disturbing a burglary

6 August

25 August

17 September

19 September

later in the year at a rematch in New Orleans, Louisiana. As an amateur, Ali (formerly Cassius Clay) won 108 fights and lost eight. Professionally, he won 56 bouts out of 61. On the subject of sport – in the University Boat Race, the Cambridge boat suffered a terrible sinking feeling. They kept rowing as the water poured in but, not surprisingly, Oxford won.

Above: Muhammad Ali arriving in Britain with his third wife, Veronica, in February 1978.

Anna Ford

Anna Ford studied at Manchester University and became President of its Students' Union. She graduated with an honours degree in Economics and, after working as a staff tutor for the Open University in Northern Ireland, joined Granada Television in Manchester as a researcher. Anna become a reporter on their evening news programme, *Granada Reports*. She later moved to the BBC and worked on the documentary series *Man Alive* before taking over from Raymond Baxter as main presenter on the popular science programme *Tomorrow's World*. In 1978 she moved to ITN and, within two months of her arrival, became the first female presenter on *News at Ten*. In 1981 she moved to the ITV breakfast programme, *TV-am*. After being sacked from the struggling station, she hit the headlines for throwing a glass of wine over MP Jonathan Aitken at a party. He was a shareholder in *TV-am* and Anna believed he was behind her dismissal. She moved back to the BBC in 1986, to present the *Six O'Clock News*, and became presenter of the *One O'Clock News* when it was relaunched in 1999. In 2003 she received a Doctorate from Queen's University, Belfast, in recognition of her services to journalism, and in 2004 the Queen presented her with the royal charter for the formal establishment of the University of Manchester.

Above: Cambridge keep on rowing in the best British tradition, as they slowly sink in the Boat Race.

Pope John Paul I dies after 38 days in office

Pope John Paul II takes office

Jonestown mass suicide of 913 People's Temple followers

The Times is suspended until November 13th 1979 due to industrial action

28 September

16 October

18 November

30 November

1979 Winter of Discontent

Above: A makeshift outdoor newsroom during the ITV strike.

Above: Ayatollah Khomeini during his exile in Paris.

The nation was hit by a wave of strikes by council workers – over the Labour government's decision to limit pay rises to five percent. ITN covered the mounting piles of rubbish on street corners and in parks, the hospitals turning away patients, the shortages of food and petrol and even the reports that grave diggers were striking and the dead could not be buried. Later in the year, ITN was itself hit by a strike and the whole of ITV was off the air for 13 weeks from August to October in a row about pay. Programmes were replaced by a blue card that carried a message, in white letters, apologising for the temporary loss of service. The first ITN programme back on the air was the *News at 5.45*. Leonard Parkin opened the programme with these words: 'Good evening. It's nice to be back. Now let's get on with it'.

There were strikes too and other civil unrest in Iran – where supporters of the exiled Iranian spiritual leader Ayatollah Khomeini were trying to overthrow the Shah. The Shah and his wife fled first to Egypt but eventually to the United States. His departure was greeted by rapture on the streets of the capital Tehran and ITN reporter Martyn Lewis was among the celebrating crowds. Many held up pictures of the Ayatollah and even the Iranian armed forces joined the clamour.

It wasn't long before the Ayatollah returned. The scenes then, reported by John Suchet, were remarkable. Huge crowds turned out to see Khomeini fly in from Paris after 14 years in exile.

Left: The Ayatollah was the spiritual leader of Iran, but had been banned from the country for 14 years.

The Shah of Iran is deposed and flees to Egypt with his family

Ayatollah Khomeini returns to Iran from exile in Paris

43 million viewers watch *Elvis!* on television, starring Kurt Russell as Elvis

Ronald Reagan starts his campaign for the Presidency

16 January   1 February   11 February   March

In late 1978, Vietnam had invaded Cambodia. The Cambodian army was easily defeated and Phnom Penh, the capital, fell in January 1979. Pol Pot and the Khmer Rouge fled to Thailand – during their radical communist regime, millions of people had been executed, or had died of starvation or illness.

Above left: The Ayatollah returned in triumph to Iran after the Shah had fled the country.

Far left: ITN reporter John Suchet was on the scene in Tehran to describe events to viewers.

Above right: Pol Pot.

Radiation escapes during a crisis at Three Mile Island nuclear power station in Pennsylvania

Airey Neave murdered by IRA car bomb in House of Commons car park

Margaret Thatcher wins the general election to become Britain's first female prime minister

Alien, starring Tom Skerritt and Sigourney Weaver, is released

28 March   30 March   4 May   25 May

1979 Politics

Right: Margaret Thatcher becomes Britain's first female prime minister.

Far right: Ronald Reagan begins his campaign for presidency of the United States.

Above: Pope John Paul II kisses the ground of his native Poland, as he becomes the first Pope to visit a communist country.

When the general election campaign was announced, the Conservative leader Margaret Thatcher told ITN's Michael Brunson, 'I'm just a little bit fearful that people might get fed up with us before the end of the campaign and I think what's important is that you finish strongly.' And indeed she did. The political landscape of Britain changed; there was a difference of two million votes between Conservative and Labour – although the Conservative majority was only 43. Mrs Thatcher – a grocer's daughter – had become Britain's first woman prime minister, and set about reducing the power of Britain's trade unions, after the winter of discontent.

As she arrived in Downing Street she told waiting reporters she was very excited and very aware of the responsibilities, exclaiming: 'This is the greatest honour that can come to any citizen. Some words of Francis of Assisi which I think really just particularly capture the moment: where there is discord may we bring harmony; where there is error may we bring

Pope John Paul II becomes the first Pope to visit a communist country when he returns to his native Poland

Gossamer Albatross becomes first man-powered machine to cross the Channel

Saddam Hussein becomes President of Iraq

Start of an 11-week technician's strike which affects the whole ITV network except for the Channel Isles

2 June

12 June

16 July

10 August

truth; where there is doubt may we bring faith; and where there is despair may we bring hope. To all the British people, how so ever they voted, may I say this; now that the election is over, may we get together and strive to serve and strengthen the country of which we are so proud to be a part. Finally, in the words of Airey Neave, whom we had hoped to bring here with us, there is now work to be done'.

Airey Neave had been Mrs Thatcher's close friend, adviser and the Conservatives' spokesman on Northern Ireland. He was murdered by the Irish National Liberation Army, earlier that year, on March 30th. A car bomb went off as he drove out of the Palace of Westminster, triggered by mercury tipping inside the device as his Vauxhall Cavalier went up the ramp out of the MPs' car park beneath the courtyard outside Westminster Hall. The assassination was seen as an attempt by republican terrorists to influence the outcome of the election and to try and force whoever became Prime Minister to pull troops out of Northern Ireland.

Below left: Police outside Westminster Hall, in the courtyard above the underground car park where Airey Neave was assassinated by an IRA bomb.

Below right: Airey Neave's wrecked car is removed from the scene.

Mr Neave's death was a serious blow for security at the Houses of Parliament and for Mrs Thatcher personally. Privately devastated, she summed up her reaction in public with these words: 'He was one of freedom's warriors. Courageous, staunch, true. He lived for his beliefs and now he has died for them'.

Lord Mountbatten murdered by IRA

Iran hostage crisis – 13 Americans are held in the US Embassy in Tehran

Pink Floyd release their album *The Wall*

Russia invades Afghanistan

27 August

November

30 November

25 December

1980s

The 1980s were the decade of the first video cameras. Electronic News Gathering, or ENG, gradually replaced film. Now it was possible to film an event and start editing the pictures straight away, without waiting for negatives to be developed. Mobile satellite dishes meant reporters could travel with the action on a moving story. And ITN expanded, in size and scope, with the launch of *Channel 4 News*.

Above: A pair of SAS marksmen on the balcony waiting for the terrorists to show.

Above: The dramatic pictures of black-clad SAS men were captured by an ITN camera secretly set up in a flat opposite.

The Iranian embassy siege provided dramatic viewing and ITN's coverage meant viewers got a unique view of its even more dramatic ending. It began in May when six armed Iranian dissidents occupied the embassy building in Kensington, taking 19 hostages including a policeman, PC Trevor Lock, and threatening to kill them if their demands were not met. The Iranians belonged to group opposed to the regime of the Ayatollah Khomeini and demanded the release of 91 political prisoners held in Tehran. A unit of SAS commandos was brought in on the sixth day of the siege, following the murder of the Iranian Press attaché, Abbas Lavasani, whose body was dumped on the Embassy steps. The terrorists threatened to shoot another hostage every 30 minutes. It was then that the Home Secretary William Whitelaw ordered the SAS to storm the building.

On that final day, ITN had managed to set up a camera in a flat that overlooked the back of the Embassy – unknown to the other media. When Mr Whitelaw's order came, ITN was able to broadcast the end of the siege, live, in the most dramatic style possible. ITN broke into the ITV schedule at 7.27pm for a newsflash that ended up lasting 40 minutes. The ITN camera showed the masked SAS men abseiling from the roof, smashing their way through the windows as strategically placed explosives were detonated.

From inside the building came the sound of gunshots as the Iranian terrorists shot dead one of their hostages and wounded another. The dramatic sequence lasted for 11 minutes – reporter Jeremy Hands beginning the commentary in the studio before his colleague Anthony Carthew reached the scene and took over. The newsflash got its own mention in that week's viewing figures – 11 million people had watched it. It also won an award from the Royal Television Society.

ITN's Silver Jubilee was marked by a Royal Visit. The Queen and the Duke of Edinburgh dropped in on the *News at Ten* studio. When newscaster Anna

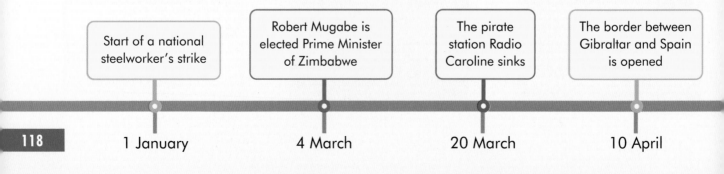

Start of a national steelworker's strike	Robert Mugabe is elected Prime Minister of Zimbabwe	The pirate station Radio Caroline sinks	The border between Gibraltar and Spain is opened
1 January	4 March	20 March	10 April

Selina Scott

· · · · · · · · · · · · · · ·

Selina Scott became a newsreader on *News at Ten* in May 1981. She had worked previously as a reporter and newsreader for Grampian Television in Scotland. She partnered Sandy Gall and Alastair Burnet, and rapidly established herself as a celebrity in her own right. She co-presented ITN's coverage of the wedding of the Prince of Wales to Lady Diana Spencer and, during the Falklands conflict, she received sufficient military fan mail to earn her the title of 'The Forces' Sweetheart'. Moving to the BBC in 1982, she helped to launch *Breakfast Time* with Frank Bough and then presented *The Clothes Show*. She was a regular guest presenter of the *Wogan* chat show on BBC1. She presented a series of documentaries on royalty, including *A Prince Among The Islands*, about Prince Charles, and *The Return Of The King*, about King Constantine's first visit to Greece for 25 years. Moving to the United States, she worked on *West 57*, a current affairs roundup, and, by 1995, she had her own show on NBC's European Superchannel that was produced in England. She presented LWT's *Eye Spy* and also worked for Sky TV. She is a regular columnist for a Sunday newspaper.

Above: A plume of smoke from inside the building, after stun grenades were lobbed in through a window.

Above: The terrorists surrender, waving a white flag, but a few moments later flames burst out of one of the windows.

Ford was introduced, she had to explain to the Queen that she couldn't stand up as she had been wired up with her earpiece, ready for the programme. If she had followed normal etiquette, the masking tape securing the wires down the back of her dress might have come unstuck.

US troops fail to rescue US diplomats held hostage by Iran

Alfred Hitchcock dies

SAS rescue 18 of the 19 hostages held by terrorists in the Iranian Embassy in London

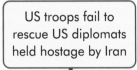

24–25 April

29 April

5 May

Above: The Queen takes tea with King Hassan of Jordan during a Royal visit to Morocco.

Right: During the war between Iran and Iraq, ITN newsman Jon Snow was directly involved in the daring rescue of British seamen.

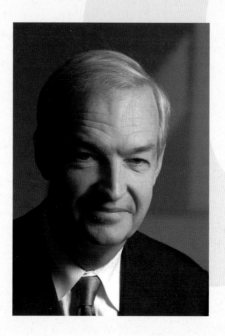

The Iran-Iraq war developed a British dimension, soon after it started in 1980, when a British cargo ship, *Atlantin*, was trapped in the fighting for six weeks in the Shatt al Arab waterway between Iran and Iraq. ITN's Jon Snow became directly involved in a daring – and successful – rescue attempt.

On board the *Atlantin* were British sailors and their wives and Filipino crewmen. The British owner of the boat had been telephoning the Foreign Office for weeks to ask for help in freeing the boat. The Foreign Office apparently told him that it wasn't in the waterway and must have moved on. Then one night the boat's owner was watching *News at Ten* when he saw the *Atlantin* over Jon's shoulder in his report. He rang ITN to ask if there was any way Jon could help his crew.

Using information supplied by the owner, Jon was able to contact a Norwegian ship in the area, which was in coded radio contact once a day with the *Atlantin*. Jon agreed to swim out to the ship at low tide so he and an Iraqi contact put on wetsuits and fins and set off. But having misunderstood the timing of the low tide they got caught in the swirling currents and were nearly swept into the line of Iranian fire. When they did make it on board the *Atlantin*, they agreed to give a signal the following evening for the ship to

Mount St. Helens erupts in Washington State, USA

Release of the second Star Wars film, *Episode V – The Empire Strikes Back*, starring Harrison Ford, Mark Hamill and Carrie Fisher

Royal visit to Morocco where the Queen meets King Hassan

18 May

21 May

October

lower its life rafts and get the people off. It was one of the first times the new electronic cameras – with their superior night time capabilities – had been used on a foreign assignment. Had it been a film camera, ITN viewers would never have seen crew clambering off the ship. Jon's coverage of the story helped win him that year's Reporter of the Year award.

At the end of the year, in New York, John Lennon was shot and killed on the steps of the apartment block in the city where he lived. The murderer was Mark David Chapman, a troubled 25 year-old Texan. He shot the star five times at close range, after stalking him for three days. Initially, ITN relied on coverage from its American partner, CBS News, but reporter Norman Rees was soon at the scene, talking to police officers about what happened and to the hospital doctors about the emergency surgery involved in trying to save Lennon's life.

Above: Lady Diana Spencer began to feature in the news, amidst reports that she was about to marry the world's most eligible bachelor, Prince Charles.

Left: John Lennon with Yoko Ono in London in 1968. The world was stunned by news of his death at the hands of a crazed gunman.

Lady Diana Spencer is in the news amidst speculation that she will marry Prince Charles

Abba release their album *Super Trouper*

100 million people tune in to find out who shot JR in the 1979–80 *Dallas* season finale

John Lennon is shot dead by a crazed fan outside the Dakota building in New York

November

3 November

21 November

8 December

Above: The funeral of IRA hunger-striker Bobby Sands in Northern Ireland.

Above middle: The coffin was followed by family members, including Bobby's young son Gerald.

Above right: Masked men in military uniform carry the coffin.

Twenty-five days after being elected as MP for Fermanagh and South Tyrone, the IRA hunger striker Bobby Sands died in the Maze Prison. He'd been refusing food for 66 days in protest against the Government. He had been involved in the 'dirty protests' in which prisoners, sickened by the beatings routinely meted out to them by prison officers when they left their cells to 'slop out', simply stopped doing so and smeared their excrement on the walls of their cells. Sands had been convicted of possessing firearms in September 1977, and had been sentenced to 14 years' imprisonment.

His funeral brought around 75,000 republicans onto the streets of Belfast. The IRA, knowing that television cameras would be there, turned his funeral into a show of strength. Masked IRA men in uniform flanked his cortège and fired a volley of rifle shots over his coffin. Viewers saw Sands's young son, Gerald, surrounded by the masked men around his father's coffin. Later that day, feelings spilled over. On the streets of Londonderry gangs of youths threw petrol bombs in clashes with police that lasted throughout the night.

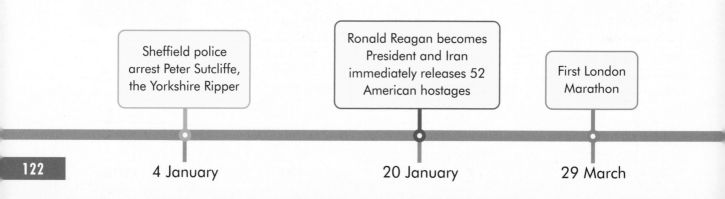

Sheffield police arrest Peter Sutcliffe, the Yorkshire Ripper

Ronald Reagan becomes President and Iran immediately releases 52 American hostages

First London Marathon

4 January

20 January

29 March

Left: A massed crowd of Roman Catholic mourners as the funeral passes a screened-off Protestant area.

On March 29th, the first London Marathon was run, over the traditional 26 miles, by nearly 8,000 people. Well over 6,000 finished. The event, modelled on the one held annually in New York, was the brainchild of Chris Brasher who, along with ITN's first newscaster, Chris Chataway, had paced Roger Bannister during his celebrated four minute mile run at Oxford's Iffley Road Stadium in 1954. The London Marathon captured the imagination of the public and now attracts more than 40,000 runners.

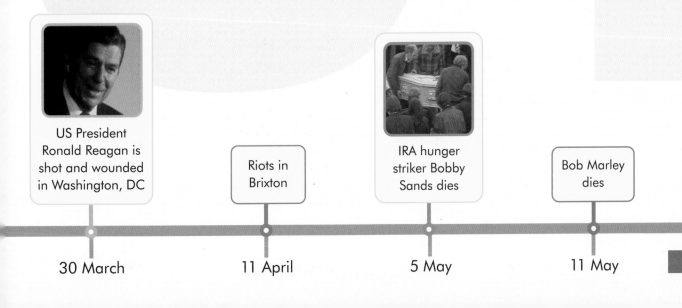

US President Ronald Reagan is shot and wounded in Washington, DC

Riots in Brixton

IRA hunger striker Bobby Sands dies

Bob Marley dies

30 March

11 April

5 May

11 May

For months the country had been in the grip of wedding fever as the marriage of Prince Charles and Lady Diana Spencer approached. ITN reporter Carol Barnes had been assigned to cover Lady Diana's movements during the build up. One celebrated television moment happened after a long wait outside Diana's flat in West London. When she did emerge, Carol and her crew were among the throng of journalists following her down the road. Carol's soundman, Nigel Thomson, was walking backwards, pointing his microphone towards the princess. Diana saw he was heading straight for a lamp post and told him to watch out. It was too late. Nigel banged into it and Diana giggled.

Above: The fairytale wedding ceremony of Lady Diana Spencer to Prince Charles, the heir to the British throne, at St Paul's Cathedral in London.

The night before the wedding, thousands of people had gathered in Hyde Park for a firework display that was supposed to start at 10pm. In fact it began a few minutes late because ITN had persuaded the organisers to delay it, so it could be carried just after the opening headlines at the start of *News at Ten*.

Carol Barnes was among the reporting team on the day of the wedding itself. Alastair Burnet and Selina Scott hosted the ITN coverage, nine hours in total. More than half a million people were on the streets of the capital, for the royal procession and the service itself at St Paul's Cathedral. Diana remembered Carol when both were pregnant the following year and sent her a telegram saying: 'From one lady in waiting to another, congratulations'.

Six weeks before the wedding, there was a security alert involving the Queen, at the Trooping the Colour ceremony. A 17-year-old called Marcus Serjeant fired six blank rounds from a replica pistol at the Queen as she

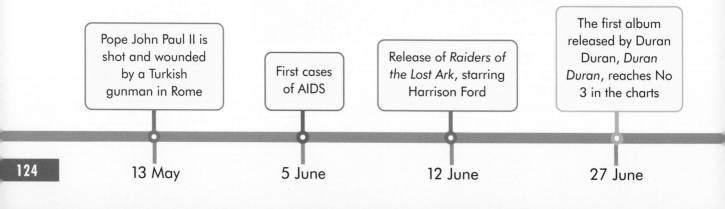

Pope John Paul II is shot and wounded by a Turkish gunman in Rome

First cases of AIDS

Release of *Raiders of the Lost Ark*, starring Harrison Ford

The first album released by Duran Duran, *Duran Duran*, reaches No 3 in the charts

13 May

5 June

12 June

27 June

rode towards Horseguards Parade. Her horse shied but she quickly brought it back under control and the ceremony continued as scheduled. Serjeant was tried and imprisoned for five years under the Treason Act of 1842.

Across the Atlantic, President Reagan was far less lucky when someone fired at him. He was hit by a would-be assassin as he left the Washington Hilton Hotel where he had been addressing a meeting. A number of pistol shots were fired by 25-year-old John Hinckley, the son of an oil executive. The President was struck by a bullet which punctured one of his lungs, White House Press Secretary John Brady was seriously wounded in the head and a policeman and a secret service agent were also wounded. President Reagan made a speedy recovery. Hinckley was found not guilty of attempting to assassinate the President on the grounds of insanity and committed to an institution.

Above: President Ronald Reaggon who survived an assassination attempt whilst in power.

Pope John Paul II was also the victim of an assassination attempt but he, like President Reagan, survived. On May 13th a Turkish gunman, Mehmet Ali Agca, shot and seriously wounded the Pope in St Peter's Square in Rome. Television pictures from the scene showed the Pope being rushed to hospital, badly wounded, leaving a shocked crowd behind him. Agca was sentenced to life imprisonment. At Christmas, in 1983, the Pope went to visit Agca in prison and spoke to him for some time in private.

Above: Pope John Paul II was also the victim of an attempted assassination, and like Ronald Reagan he survived.

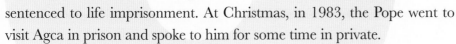

Gunman fires eight blanks at Queen Elizabeth II during the Trooping the Colour ceremony

Wedding of Prince Charles and Diana

Egyptian President Anwar Sadat assassinated

30 June

29 July

6 October

Above: Argentinian planes attacked and hit British ships in Bluff Cove during the Falklands War.

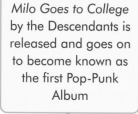

Above: Survivors of the attack at Bluff Cove come ashore by lifeboat.

The Falklands War was a defining moment in modern British history and in the history of television news. Reporting a battle on the other side of the world brought massive logistical challenges, many of which ITN overcame. Few had heard of the Falklands before Argentina invaded – yet within a few weeks the name was seared into the psyche of the nation.

Sovereignty of the Falklands had been disputed since the mid 18th century. To divert his people's attention away from a looming economic crisis, General Leopoldo Galtieri, head of Argentina's military junta, decided to reclaim the islands. They lay some 8,000 miles from Britain, which had shown little interest in protecting them. But General Galtieri had reckoned without Margaret Thatcher. In the early stages of the Falklands crisis, she gave an interview to ITN and was asked if she would resign if she failed to reclaim the islands. 'Failure?' she retorted. 'The possibility does not exist'.

ITN camera teams were on *HMS Hermes*, one of two aircraft carriers in the 40-vessel task force. Ministry of Defence officials only allowed ITN to put a satellite dish on one of its ships because they believed it would be impossible to transmit from it. But by the time they had reached Ascension Island, the ITN engineer on board had worked out a way of sending live pictures. The MOD was so amazed at what he'd managed to do that he was asked to leave the ship – with all his gear – at Ascension Island.

The battle for the islands was bloody and vicious. 250 British servicemen, and 652 Argentinian troops lost their lives. The terrible events of war unfolded in the homes of millions of people although there was a time lag in reports reaching the screen, partly due to the difficulty in getting pictures back to London but also because the MOD insisted on seeing reports before they were broadcast to make sure no sensitive information went out.

Milo Goes to College by the Descendants is released and goes on to become known as the first Pop-Punk Album

Mark Thatcher, son of the Prime Minister, disappears in the Sahara during the Paris-Dakar rally but is rescued 3 days later

Laker Airways collapses, leaving 6,000 passengers stranded

Pope John Paul II visits Britain

1 January 11 January 5 February May

The most harrowing images resulted from an air attack on two Royal Fleet Auxiliaries, *Sir Tristram* and *Sir Galahad*, at San Carlos Bay. As soldiers and crewmen came ashore, many of them seriously wounded and badly burned, the events were described, vividly, by ITN's Michael Nicholson.

Above: British troops advancing towards Port Stanley.

Jon Snow

Jon Snow has been the main presenter of *Channel 4 News* since 1989. He worked in local radio before joining ITN in 1976. He became Washington correspondent in 1984, returning to London two years later to take up the post of Diplomatic Editor. His dramatic reporting style has won him many admirers and many awards for his work in places such as Eritrea, Afghanistan, Iran, Iraq and El Salvador. He received awards from the Royal Television Society for his work in Poland in 1979, for Afghanistan, Iran and the Middle East in 1980, and for El Salvador twice, in 1981 and 1982. There have been awards too for his work on *Channel 4 News*. He was News Presenter of the Year in 2003 and received a BAFTA the following year. Jon reported on the fall of the Berlin Wall, the release of Nelson Mandela from prison, the Pope's visit to Poland and the Columbia shuttle disaster. In 1999, he interviewed Monica Lewinsky for Channel 4's *Dispatches*. Jon has also presented *First Edition*, a news and current affairs roundup aimed at teenagers.

Above: One soldier makes absolutely sure everyone knows what side he is on, with a Union Jack attached to his radio set aerial.

Argentinian forces surrender when Port Stanley is recaptured by the British

Battle of Port Stanley in the Falklands War

Argentina invades the Falkland Islands, start of the Falklands War

E.T. the Extra-Terrestrial, starring Drew Barrymore, is released

31 May

2 April

11 June

14 June

ITN ITN ITN ITN

Channel 4 News

Right: Princess Diana and the Prince of Wales emerge from St Mary's Hospital in Paddington with the baby Prince William.

Above: The *Channel Four News* team, which included specialist journalists and some well-known ITV faces.

Above: The Prince and Princess of Wales on holiday in Scotland just after their wedding.

ITN's coming of age as a truly independent supplier of news was in 1982 with the launch of *Channel Four News*. It was a big challenge for ITN, to prove it could produce an hour-long programme that was distinctive from its bulletins on ITV. Its brief was to be analytical, specialist and give more weight to international news, politics and the economy. Some specialist journalists were hired to cover foreign affairs, the arts and science. Some ITV faces were given the opportunity to show what they could do within lengthier reports. Peter Sissons moved from ITN's *News at One* to present the programme, assisted by Trevor McDonald. There was initially a tacit policy that there was no place for ITV-type stories on the royal family, sport, film stars and crimes of violence. There were some teething troubles in the first few months and some of the guiding principles changed. But more than 20 years on, *Channel Four News* has earned a reputation and awards for innovative, in-depth journalism, and acquired very healthy ratings.

Because Prince William was born more than four months before *Channel Four News*, there was no dilemma at ITN about how much coverage to give the story. ITN reporters joined the throng of journalists camped outside St Mary's Hospital in Paddington, waiting for news. When Prince Charles left the hospital, he said he was 'relieved and delighted'. The baby was on 'marvellous form'. As for names, he and Diana had thought of one or two

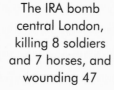

Prince William is born

The IRA bomb central London, killing 8 soldiers and 7 horses, and wounding 47

Greenham Common Peace Camp founded

Princess Grace of Monaco killed in a car crash

21 June   20 July   September   13 September

but there was, as the Prince put it, 'a bit of an argument' about that. Diana was thought to favour more modern names like Sebastian or Oliver. For several days the name game continued, with the new addition to the most famous family in the world known only as 'Baby Wales'.

As Charles left the hospital he appealed to journalists and well-wishers outside not to make too much noise. 'Sleep is badly needed in there', he said.

There was more ground breaking journalism for ITN with the visit of the Pope to Britain, the first such visit for 450 years. Normally outside broadcasts of events of national importance were mounted by Thames Television – the ITV station then covering London – but this time ITN was to play the lead role. John Paul II had been Pope for four years and was at the height of his charismatic powers. The trip had been in danger of cancellation due to the Falklands War and during his visit His Holiness spoke out against the conflict.

At Greenham Common, near Newbury in Berkshire, the first women arrived to set up camp in non-violent protest, calling for nuclear disarmament across the world. Greenham Common had once been common land, but had been taken over as an airbase by the RAF during World War II. After the war it became one of three UK bases of the US Strategic Air Command, who left in 1964. However, in the late seventies it was decided to install 96 cruise missiles there – with another 64 at RAF Molesworth – to counter the perceived threat of a Russian nuclear strike. The peace camp – which was for women only – drew worldwide attention to the growing peace movement.

Top left and right: Women press up against the fence at Greenham Common Airbase, protesting about cruise missiles being stationed on British soil.

Middle: The Peace Camp had a floating population – some came when they could, others lived there for long periods.

Bottom: Sarah Hipperson, one of the Greenham Common women, is interviewed in 2000 about her memories of the cruise missile protests.

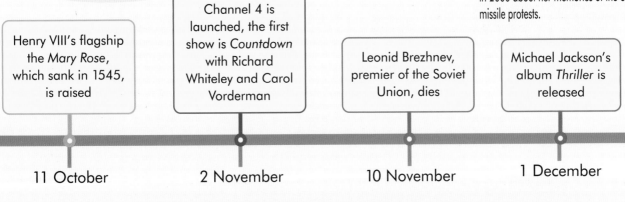

Henry VIII's flagship the *Mary Rose*, which sank in 1545, is raised

Channel 4 is launched, the first show is *Countdown* with Richard Whiteley and Carol Vorderman

Leonid Brezhnev, premier of the Soviet Union, dies

Michael Jackson's album *Thriller* is released

11 October

2 November

10 November

1 December

R iding high on a wave of national relief and some rejoicing at Britain's victory over Argentina in the Falklands, Margaret Thatcher swept to a second-term victory in the General Election. ITN pioneered a new approach to covering the movements and musings of the three main party leaders. Separate teams, called target teams, would cover each leader throughout the campaign. Michael Brunson was to follow Mrs Thatcher. David Rose would report on Labour leader Michael Foot. Alastair Stewart would cover the campaign of the Liberal leader, David Steel. Now all the major broadcasters cover elections in this way – but at the time it had never been done before.

Below: In 1983 Margaret Thatcher, left, swept to victory in the General Election after the success of the previous year's Falklands campaign, right.

The Labour Party's election manifesto, accurately described by one of their own senior MPs as 'the longest suicide note in history', put forward a robustly left-wing agenda, which misjudged the mood of the country. The result was never really in doubt, so ITN decided it needed something

Seatbelts become mandatory for front seat passengers in the UK

TV-AM launched

Worst-ever bush fires in Australia claim 71 lives

Deidre Barlow returns to her husband Ken in *Coronation Street*, in one of the highest-rated episodes in the serial's history

31 January

1 February

16 February

23 February

a bit special to make the election night programme more exciting and asked whether it might be possible to place a miniature camera in the back of Mrs Thatcher's car, taking her from her constituency count in Finchley, to Downing Street. It could beam back live pictures of her. Mrs Thatcher's press officers liked the idea and so did the lady herself. She did have one question though – how could she tell when it was transmitting? She wouldn't like viewers to be able to see her scratching her nose, for example. There was concern at ITN that if she was given a button to switch it off, she might forget to switch it back on again in the excitement of the night. As ever, the simplest solution proved the best. She was given a piece of black velvet that she could place across the lens, if she needed to. In fact she never did and the pictures were the highlight of the night's programme.

Above: Lech Walesa spends a quiet moment away from the public eye, enjoying a spot of fishing.

While the power of the unions was under threat in Britain, in Poland they were growing stronger. Lech Walesa, an electrician working in the Lenin shipyard at Gdansk, had become the leader of the Solidarity movement and faced down the communist authorities. In this he was probably as instrumental in the collapse of communism in Europe as were his fellow Pole, Pope John Paul II, and Soviet leader Mikhail Gorbachev.

Above: Lech Walesa's stand against communists in Poland as leader of the Solidarity movement began a process which led to the collapse of the Soviet Block in Eastern Europe.

Prince Charles and Diana tour Australia and New Zealand

Bob Hawke is elected Prime Minister of Australia

Michael Jackson performs the Moonwalk dance step for the first time, while recording 'Billie Jean' for a Motown TV special, to be aired on 16 May

US Embassy in Beirut is bombed amidst continuing unrest between the PLO and Syrian-backed rebels

March

5 March

25 March

18 April

Above: An old woman in Baddawi refuge camp in Tripoli in Lebanon covers her ears as Syrian-backed rebels fire rockets at PLO troops nearby, who retaliate with rockets of their own.

Right: Rebel fighters pose for the cameras.

Far right: One of the rockets hits a block of nearby flats.

The most dangerous location on earth in the early 1980s was Beirut and it was the place to be for reporters wanting to make a name for themselves. Most of the city had been reduced to rubble as the country had descended into a bloody and confusing civil war between various militias. Yasser Arafat, leader of the Palestinian Liberation Organisation, was able to exploit the chaos to create a state-within-a-state, as he had previously done in Jordan. Reporters from all over the world covered Beirut's descent into anarchy, as the fighting raged, bloodily, ceaselessly and pointlessly about them. At one stage, an ITN crew was held hostage, blamed for the death of their own driver, but were released after the payment of a substantial ransom. But ITN reporters and crews continued to risk their lives to report the story.

The Royal Family was on the move. The Queen, accompanied by the Duke of Edinburgh, visited Canada and the United States, having first opened the Jamaican parliament in its 21st year. The Royal party was warmly received by President Reagan and his wife, Nancy, and visited their ranch in California. They also took a trip to Hollywood. Later in the

Wheel clamps on illegally-parked cars are introduced by London police

The third Star Wars film, *Episode VI – Return of the Jedi*, starring Mark Hamill, Harrison Ford and Carrie Fisher, is released

Mass outbreak from the Maze prison

Lech Walesa, leader of Solidarity, wins the Nobel Prize for Peace

16 May

25 May

23 September

October

Far left: The Prince of Wales reads a speech during the Royal couple's tour of Australia.

Left: Princess Diana during an official function at Government House during the tour of New Zealand.

Below left: Prince Charles bursts into laughter as Princess Diana tells the pupils of an Australian radio 'school of the airwaves' that Prince William likes to play with his 'little balls... that blow out of the top of his favourite toy plastic whale'.

Below right: Princess Diana and Prince Charles on walkabout.

year they travelled to Sweden and to Kenya – where the Queen visited the famous Treetops Hotel, at which she had been staying when she received the news of the death of her father, King George VI. In November, during a visit to Bangladesh and India, the Queen presented Mother Theresa of Calcutta with the insignia of the Order of Merit.

The Prince and Princess of Wales visited Australia and New Zealand, during which support for the monarchy, which had been waning, received a massive boost, partly due to the Diana phenomenon but also to their young son. Prince William spent much of the tour out of the limelight – being looked after by his nanny Barbara Barnes. But ITN cameras made the most of their chances to film Prince William – particularly when he was allowed to roam around on a rug in New Zealand while his parents posed, once again, for the cameras. Wherever the royal couple went, they were big news and crowds turned up to welcome them.

Truck bomb destroys US Marine Corps barracks at Beirut Airport, killing 241 servicemen

First Cruise missiles arrive at Greenham Common

Brinks Mat robbery - £26 million in gold bars is stolen from Heathrow

Harrods bombed by IRA, killing 6 and injuring 90

23 October

13 November

26 November

17 December

Above: Reggie Bosanquet

There was sad news at ITN – with the death, from cancer, of Reggie Bosanquet. He was only 51. A memorial service was held for him, attended by friends and former colleagues. His *News at Ten* presenting partner Andrew Gardner summed up the occasion. 'This is not a solemn service of remembrance,' he said. 'Rather it is a celebration of Reggie and an occasion to look back on the fond memories with laughter'.

On September 15th at 4.20pm, Diana, Princess of Wales, gave birth to her second son: Henry Charles Albert David – to be known as Harry – at St Mary's Hospital, Paddington. He weighed 6 lb 14 oz and was third in line to the throne. ITN cameras were there when he and his mother left hospital and covered what celebrations there were – for example, the bell ringing at the Church in Tetbury, close to Highgrove, the couple's country home. But the mood of the country was different to that when Prince William was born. William was the heir, Harry the 'spare'. ITN filmed as Harry arrived home at Kensington Palace and then again as Prince Charles left home later that day. Charles was dressed in his polo gear and off to a match. The royal routine continued, despite the new arrival.

Harry was christened by the Archbishop of Canterbury, Dr Robert Runcie, at St George's Chapel, Windsor on December 21st.

Apple releases the Macintosh

Miner's strike begins

Colin Baker becomes the new Doctor in *Doctor Who*

22 January

12 March

16 March

Elinor Goodman

Elinor Goodman was Political Editor for *Channel 4 News* from 1988 to July 2005. Elinor joined *Channel 4 News* as Political Correspondent in 1982 after eleven years at the *Financial Times*.

Elinor has a formidable reputation as a political pundit, with her skilful reporting and analysis of the twists and turns of Government. During her 23 years at *Channel 4 News*, she has covered six General Elections, countless by-elections and a host of European elections.

Elinor began her career in journalism in the late 60's on the advertising trade magazine, *Campaign*. She was appointed a reporter after working on the publication as a secretary.

In 1970 she joined the City Office of the *Daily Telegraph* where she spent a year reporting on all aspects of media and marketing. Moving on in 1971 Elinor spent the next eleven years working for the *Financial Times* – first as Consumer Affairs Correspondent, and then as Political Correspondent.

Above: Prince Harry hides from his public, snuggled inside a warm woolly blanket.

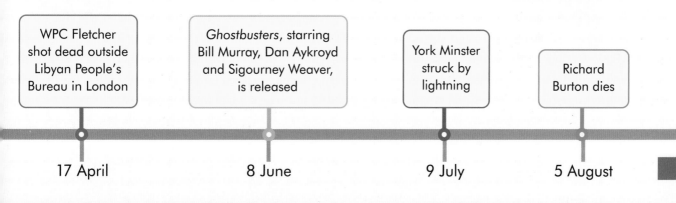

WPC Fletcher shot dead outside Libyan People's Bureau in London	*Ghostbusters*, starring Bill Murray, Dan Aykroyd and Sigourney Weaver, is released	York Minster struck by lightning	Richard Burton dies
17 April	8 June	9 July	5 August

1984 Politics

Above left: Arthur Scargill, leader of the National Union of Mineworkers, took his workers into a strike to try and defend the future of mining in Britain.

Above middle: Violent clashes between mineworkers and police outside the Orgreave coking plant.

Above right: The strike ultimately ended in defeat for the miners.

Opposite left: Mrs Thatcher interviewed after the Brighton bomb.

Opposite middle: The bomb wrecked the Grand Hotel in Brighton, which was hosting the Conservative Party Conference.

Opposite right: One of the survivors is dramatically rescued from the rubble.

The miners' strike brought hardship, division and violence to pit communities around the country. Britain's industrial and social fabric unravelled in front of the television cameras. It was an epic struggle – both human and political. The leader of the National Union of Mineworkers, Arthur Scargill, believed his industry was under attack by the Coal Board and Margaret Thatcher's government and was determined to resist. There were regular confrontations between strikers and police. The ugliest took place at the Orgreave coking plant, near Rotherham in South Yorkshire. On one day at the end of May, 69 people were injured there and 82 arrested. Mounted police were used. The next month, Arthur Scargill was among 79 people arrested.

The strike provided perhaps the first real opportunity for *Channel 4 News* to show just how different it could be. It persuaded Mr Scargill and the chairman of the Coal Board, Ian MacGregor to make their own film reports, putting across their cases. They ran on consecutive days. It is a technique that has been used many times since in contentious disputes, but it was a first for British television news. The following day, the two men appeared together in the studio for a compelling debate. *Channel 4 News* won many supporters among the miners themselves. Often the crews

Prince Harry is born

IRA bomb the Grand Hotel, Brighton, during the Conservative Party conference

Michael Buerk's report on the Ethiopian famine prompts Bob Geldof to Live Aid

Indira Gandhi is assassinated

15 September   12 October   24 October   31 October

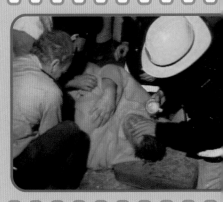

working for ITV or for BBC TV news were turned on by angry miners who felt their case wasn't being accurately portrayed by the two main channels. But when crews said they were working for *Channel 4 News* the miners were usually happy for them to film them and their communities.

A far more sinister political conflict brought death and damage to the Grand Hotel in Brighton, the base for the Conservative party leadership during their party conference. An IRA bomb, fitted with a timing device, had been placed behind a wall panel in a bathroom, to coincide with Mrs Thatcher's stay. It went off in the early hours of the morning. The Prime Minister herself was in her room at the time, apparently working on her main conference speech. She wasn't injured but dozens of others were and four people were killed including Sir Anthony Berry, one of her MPs.

Abroad, India dominated the headlines. In June, ITN had covered the storming of the Golden Temple at Amritsar by Indian troops. Some 250 Sikh extremists who had been occupying the temple complex were killed. On October 31st, India's Prime Minister, Indira Ghandi, was assassinated by some of her Sikh bodyguards, apparently in response to the attack on their sacred shrine. On December 3rd, a gas leak at the Union Carbide plant in Bhopal caused the death of some 20,000 people.

Above: The body of Indian Prime Minister Indira Gandhi is placed on her funeral pyre, amidst scenes of national grief.

Metallica release their album *Ride the Lightning*

Gas leak at Bhopal in India kills 3,800 people

Beverly Hills Cop, starring Eddie Murphy, is released

16 November

3 December

5 December

Right: The wreck of the British Airtours Boeing 737 at Manchester International Airport.

Above: Fireman wade through a sea of foam around the plane.

On August 22nd, reports reached the newsdesk of a fire on board a plane at Manchester Airport and the ITN North of England correspondent Michael MacMillan was scrambled to go there. A packed holiday charter flight bound for Corfu had caught fire as it took off and 54 passengers were killed. Such was the speed at which the flames engulfed the British Airtours Boeing 737, that some were burned to death still strapped in their seats at the rear of the plane. 83 passengers and crew survived – some with only superficial injuries.

The fire broke out when the plane's port engine exploded. Debris punctured the wing fuel tank and escaping fuel ignited. On the flight deck, the crew were aware of nothing more than a loud bang and assumed that a tyre had punctured. The pilot aborted the take-off and swung the aircraft off the runway. Crosswinds carried the fire on to the aircraft's fuselage and within 40 seconds of engine failure, the jet was engulfed in flames. Toxic smoke filled the passenger compartment. ITN spoke to survivors in Wythenshawe hospital who described the panic that followed, with passengers trampling over one another as they desperately tried to get out.

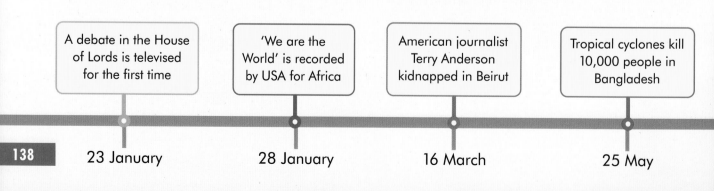

A debate in the House of Lords is televised for the first time	'We are the World' is recorded by USA for Africa	American journalist Terry Anderson kidnapped in Beirut	Tropical cyclones kill 10,000 people in Bangladesh
23 January	28 January	16 March	25 May

Above left and right: The fire in the left engine was blown against the fuselage by the crosswind, and 55 passengers lost their lives.

The miners' strike finally ended, after almost a year of misery. *Channel 4 News* broadcast a special programme covering the announcement of the result from a delegate conference of the National Union of Mineworkers, held at TUC headquarters in London. The vote was close; 98 votes to 91 in favour of ending the strike, which had lasted 355 days – not quite a year. It had divided mining communities and the country, and ended in bitterness and tears. It was a huge setback for the mineworkers' president Arthur Scargill, but with customary bravado he insisted the struggle would go on. Plans for pit closures would be contested at local level, he said.

Alastair Burnet conducted the first ever interview with the Prince and Princess of Wales since their marriage – four years earlier. ITN was allowed exclusive access to Kensington Palace and the film included footage of the two little princes. Such was the fascination with the royal couple that the programme, syndicated around the world was watched by an estimated 750 million people.

Heysel Stadium Disaster – 39 football fans die and hundreds are injured

Back to the Future, starring Michael J Fox, is released

Greenpeace ship *Rainbow Warrior* sunk in Auckland Harbour, New Zealand by French agents

29 May

3 July

10 July

Above: The *Titanic* was considered practically unsinkable when she was built, but tragically it turned out that the engineers had miscalculated.

Above: Captain Edward J. Smith, who was master of the *Titanic* on her maiden voyage.

When divers located the wreck of the *Titanic* in September, its discovery became an almost nightly story on ITN. The divers, working for a combined French and American operation, the Woods Hole Oceanographic Institute, had taken eight weeks to find the ship, ending a mystery that dated back to 1912. That was when the supposedly unsinkable passenger liner famously hit an iceberg off the Grand Banks of Newfoundland and went down with the loss of more than 1,500 lives. The oceanographers filmed the wreck, lying two and a half miles below the surface, using an unmanned submarine. The *Titanic* was the largest liner in the world when it was launched. It was supposed to ply the Atlantic route, taking passengers in luxury from Southampton across to New York.

On the day the wreck was pinpointed, ITN spoke by telephone to the expedition leader at the wreck site and obtained an interview with the diver who had led the underwater team. ITN also spoke to one of the survivors of the *Titanic* about her thoughts on the discovery of what amounted to the grave of her father who was drowned. She said she thought the wreck should be left untouched. Over the next few nights, ITN talked to salvage experts about the possibility of the wreck being raised. The consensus of opinion was that the wreck would disintegrate if it was brought to the surface. Anyway, the search team said they didn't want to disturb anything. That, they said, would amount to grave robbing. They just wanted to film the site.

Later in September, ITN covered the case, brought by a British based salvage team, at the High Court which cleared the way for the raising of the *Titanic*. The judge ruled that a British court had no jurisdiction over a wreck found in international waters. Some items were removed from the wreck and most of them are now on display at the National Maritime Museum in Greenwich.

A Boeing 737 bursts into flames after the pilot aborts take-off from Manchester International Airport, 55 are killed

Wreck of the *Titanic* discovered by American oceanographers

Live Aid concert

13 July

22 August

1 September

On October 5th, rioting on the Broadwater Farm estate broke out when police went to the home of a black woman, Cynthia Jarrett, to search her home for property which they believed had been stolen by her son. They found nothing but during the police raid, Mrs Jarrett suffered a fatal heart attack. On the morning of October 6th, members of the Jarrett family met local police to request an inquiry, making it perfectly clear that they wished to avoid any kind of disorder as a result of the incident. Bernie Grant, the leader of Haringey's council, condemned the police for the manner in which they had carried out the raid. That evening, violence flared and then exploded and the police were summoned to a disturbance on the estate at around 6.45pm. A large mob pelted them with bricks, bottles and petrol bombs, cars were set alight and shops were broken into and looted. Police reinforcements were called in and the situation deteriorated into a full-scale riot. At around 9.45pm shots were fired and a police officer was seriously wounded. Half an hour later PC Keith Blakelock was attacked. A community officer, Blakelock was hacked to death by the mob, a kitchen knife plunged into his neck up to its handle. It was the first time a police officer had been killed in a riot.

ITN camera crews put themselves in danger to cover these riots, filming as knives and bullets flew through the air. It was the first time guns had been fired by protesters in a riot in mainland Britain. A BBC camera crew was injured in the violence but no one in ITN's camera crews – who went on to win an award for their coverage – was hurt.

In 1987, three men – Mark Braithwaite, Engin Raghip and Winston Silcott – were convicted of murdering PC Blakelock, but they were cleared on appeal and released from prison four years later due to claims that evidence had been fabricated.

Above: In 1912, friends and relatives congregated outside the offices of the White Star Line for news of the disaster and to hear the fate of their loved ones. Over 1,500 people died when the *Titanic* went down – it was one of the worst peacetime maritime disasters in history.

Earthquake kills 9,000 people and destroys 95,000 homes in Mexico City

Orson Welles dies

President Ronald Reagan and Soviet premier Mikhail Gorbachev meet for the first time in Geneva

The Color Purple, starring Whoopi Goldberg and Oprah Winfrey, is released

19 September

11 October

19 November

20 December

The Queen celebrated her 60th birthday and accepted an invitation to visit the People's Republic of China. ITN saw an opportunity to produce daily special programmes from the places the Queen was visiting, in this first-ever visit to China by a British monarch. It would be relatively straightforward from somewhere like Beijing but smaller, more remote places would be difficult, and what about the historic moment the Queen set foot on the Great Wall of China? Chinese authorities eventually agreed to the idea and ITN engineers decided it could be achieved with a mobile satellite dish. No tests of the equipment would be allowed in advance so it was a gamble, but one ITN was prepared to take. A satellite dish was shipped to Beijing, slung below a Chinese army helicopter and flown to the wall. It worked. For the first time the world saw live pictures from the Great Wall of China.

Earlier in the year, the Royal Yacht *Britannia* had fulfilled her role as a Royal Naval vessel by assisting in the evacuation of refugees from Aden. Her launches picked up over 1,000 people waiting on beaches for rescue. In July, Prince Andrew, the Queen's second son, married Sarah Ferguson at Westminster Abbey and was subsequently created Duke of York.

Plans by a retired MI5 officer, Peter Wright, to publish his memoirs in Australia sent ITN reporters off to Sydney where the British Government had brought a court case to try and stop him. As a former member of the intelligence services Wright was bound to secrecy, but in the book, *Spycatcher*, he claimed that the former head of MI5, Roger Hollis, was a spy. Even before the case opened at Sydney's Supreme Court, it had cost the British taxpayer £250,000. Peter Wright died in 1995 a millionaire, thanks in part to all the publicity the court case had brought his book.

Above: Queen Elizabeth II celebrates her 60th birthday.

Above: The censorship of *Spycatcher*, the memoirs of a retired MI5 officer, did wonders for its sales.

First inductions into the Rock 'n' Roll Hall of Fame include Chuck Berry, Elvis Presley and Buddy Holly

Leon Brittan resigns from the government over the Westland affair

US space shuttle *Challenger* explodes just after lift-off, the seven astronauts are killed

23 January

24 January

28 January

There was a dramatic walk out on *Channel 4 News* by Michael Heseltine, who had resigned from the Cabinet as Defence Secretary over the Westland helicopter row. When Mr Heseltine found out the programme was planning to run a report by former civil servant, Clive Pointing, who had leaked secrets from the Ministry of Defence, he left the studio but was eventually persuaded to return.

Above: Richard Branson on the deck of his powerboat, *Virgin Atlantic Challenger II*.

Carol Barnes

● ●

Carol Barnes was managing editor of the London magazine *Time Out* and a founder member of the London Broadcasting Company. She grew up in South London before graduating from Sheffield University where she studied French and Spanish. She worked on the BBC Radio 4's *World at One* and joined ITN in 1975. As a reporter, she covered the troubles in Northern Ireland and the Brixton Riots as well as the weddings of the Prince of Wales and Lady Diana Spencer in 1981 and of Prince Andrew to Sarah Ferguson in 1986. She became a newscaster in 1979 and joined *News at Ten* in 1986. In 1984 Carol covered the US election campaign of Geraldine Ferraro, the first woman to run for the Vice Presidency. In 1989 she became the presenter of *Channel 4 Daily* before transferring to the *News at 5.40*. She has presented a fitness programme for Yorkshire TV and Meridian Television's *Seven Days* political discussion programme. She has also been a regular newscaster on the ITV *News Channel*.

Above: The millionaire businessman had just beaten the transatlantic record to take the Blue Riband award.

Halley's comet visible in northern hemisphere

Filipino President Ferdinand Marcos is deposed

A fire devastates Hampton Court Palace

British journalist John McCarthy is kidnapped in Beirut

February

25 February

31 March

17 April

For two days the world knew nothing of what was to become its worst nuclear accident. The explosion at the Chernobyl nuclear reactor near Kiev had gone unreported by the Soviet Union, which was then still practically a secret society behind its iron curtain; the fact that the Soviet Union eventually admitted to the explosion was a reflection of President Gorbachev's policy of greater openness. It was only when scientists at a nuclear plant at Forsmark in Sweden, on the Baltic coast, detected high levels of radiation in the atmosphere that anyone knew anything was wrong. At first, the Swedish scientists assumed it was their reactor which was leaking. Then came more reports of unusually high radioactivity from Stockholm and Helsinki. It was clear something terrible had happened. The story was to dominate ITN bulletins for weeks.

Below: The disaster at Chernobyl released a cloud of radiation over much of Europe.

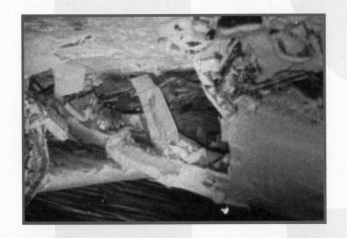

The explosion was caused by an experiment on one of Chernobyl's reactors. A series of tests was carried out, ahead of a scheduled shut-down on the night of April 25th. The tests were intended to determine how long the reactor's turbines would continue to generate energy in the event of a loss of power supply to them, although it was already known that this design of reactor could become unstable at low power settings. In the early hours of the morning of April 26th, the reactor's automatic fail-safe shut-down devices were disabled in order for the test to go ahead. As the turbines slowed, the flow of water to cool the reactor core diminished and power output increased. When an operator attempted to shut down the reactor manually, a massive power surge caused an explosion that blew the cover off the reactor, allowing burning fuel and graphite to be thrown into the air. The radioactivity released was equivalent to 40 times that of the atomic bombs dropped on Hiroshima and Nagasaki.

Queen's 60th birthday celebrations

Explosion at Chernobyl nuclear station releases a radioactive cloud across Russia and much of Europe

Top Gun, starring Tom Cruise and Kelly McGillis, is released

Maradona's 'Hand of God' knocks England out of the World Cup

21 April

26 April

16 May

22 June

31 people were killed immediately by the explosion. Of the huge labour force drafted in to extinguish the fire, clean up the contamination and erect a 'sarcophagus' of concrete and steel over the wrecked reactor, more than 6,000 have died. The United Nations estimates that almost nine million people have been affected in one way or another by the disaster. Around half a million were forced to leave their homes in the area and most have not returned. Over 160,000 square kilometres of land in Belarus, Ukraine, and Russia remain contaminated and unusable. The effects of the radiation spread as far as Britain. ITN reported how two million sheep in Wales had been contaminated with radioactivity and sheep movements and milk sales were restricted in Scotland.

Below left and right: Work by sculptor Henry Moore, who died at the end of August, 1986.

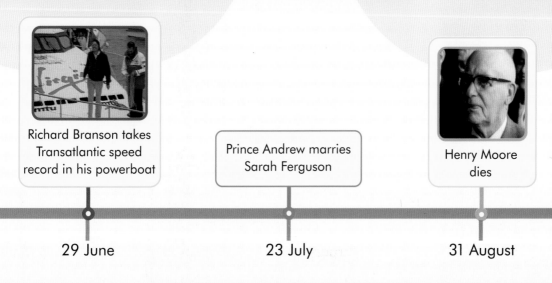

Richard Branson takes Transatlantic speed record in his powerboat

Prince Andrew marries Sarah Ferguson

Henry Moore dies

29 June

23 July

31 August

Above top and bottom: The *Herald of Free Enterprise* lies on her side in the sea off Holland, after leaving port with her bow doors still open. The accident claimed 197 lives.

Above right: Another ferry in trouble – a Sealink boat aground at Dover, victim of the October hurricane that hit southern England.

*N*ews at Ten was preparing to go on air on March 6th when reports came through of a ferry capsizing near Zeebrugge in Belgium. Those first reports, as is often the case, underestimated the scale of the disaster. As the evening wore on, it appeared that around 50 passengers had drowned. The final figure later turned out to be nearly 200, a third of those on board. All *News at Ten* had to broadcast that night was a ship-to-shore telephone interview with the captain of the rescue ship who described the terrible confusion. The first pictures to reach ITN that night came after *News at Ten* had ended. They showed ambulances at the quayside in Zeebrugge taking the survivors to hospital in the port or in Bruges.

ITN went back on air with a newsflash at 11.23pm with those pictures. It wasn't until the following morning that dawn revealed the Townsend Thoresen car ferry *Herald of Free Enterprise* lying on its side on a sandbank where it had tipped over.

It had set sail with its bow doors open, allowing water to wash through the car decks unhindered. Passengers later described hearing crashes and then an enormous bang as the water rushed to one side and tipped the ferry over.

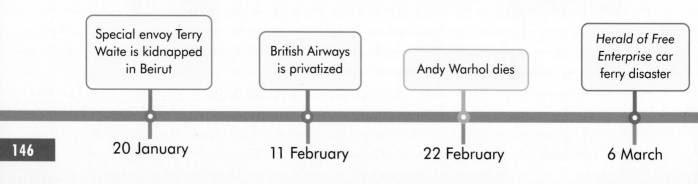

Special envoy Terry Waite is kidnapped in Beirut

British Airways is privatized

Andy Warhol dies

Herald of Free Enterprise car ferry disaster

20 January

11 February

22 February

6 March

On February 2nd, ITN launched its *World News* service. John Suchet presented the first television news service to be broadcast, via satellite, across the globe. ITN was expanding in other ways too. It opened its first bureau in Moscow. Until then the ITN teams had operated from hotel rooms, assuming they were allowed into Moscow in the first place. Reporter Ian Glover-James and picture editor Roger Pittman assembled shelves and fixed wiring to get their Soviet show on the road and succeeded in so doing by driving their edited reports out to a Moscow suburb to have them transmitted to London.

Left and below: The Iran-Iraq war lasted from September 1980 to August 1988. It began after a series of border disputes, and escalated after Iraq invaded Iran. Brent Sadler keeps ITN viewers up to date on the situation in January 1987.

Lethal Weapon, starring Mel Gibson and Danny Glover, is released

US agrees to protect Kuwaiti oil tankers during the Iran-Iraq war

Fred Astaire dies

6 March

7 March

22 June

Top: Mrs Thatcher gives her famous three-finger salute after winning a third term in office.

Middle: The jewels of the Duchess of Windsor – the former Mrs Wallis Simpson – are sold at Sothebys in Geneva. Many were given to her by her husband, the former King Edward VIII.

Mrs Thatcher was about to call an election when she gave ITN an interview about her holiday arrangements. She managed not to give anything away about her polling day plans. As the cameras rolled, she and her husband Denis flicked through their diaries. 'If we have an election early, we can go on holiday in August', Mrs Thatcher said. She went on, 'If we have an election late...' At which point Mr Thatcher butted in '...we won't go at all'. Turning to her husband, Mrs Thatcher said, 'Is Cornwall all right? You can play golf in the morning, if not in the afternoon too'. That seemed to settle it. And they got their holiday. Mrs Thatcher called the election for June 11th.

Jon Snow was assigned to cover the campaign of Labour leader Neil Kinnock for *News at Ten*. The usual logistical problems of criss-crossing the country were, on one occasion, made worse by the weather. Jon's team were trying to beam back a report from Anglesey, intended to be the main story for that night's programme. They were driving towards the satellite truck, which they could see on a hilltop, when the fog suddenly came down. They drove on at break-neck speed but were no longer clear where they were aiming. They eventually found the truck with five minutes to spare and handed the edited tape of the report to the engineer to replay to London – only when he tried to do so, he discovered that the fog had got into the equipment and it didn't work. So no top story for *News at Ten* and life and limb had been risked for nothing. Mrs Thatcher, meanwhile, went on to to become the first prime minister in over a century to win a third consecutive general election.

On August 19th at Hungerford, in Berkshire, a man called Michael Ryan killed 16 people in a random shooting spree. He was armed with an automatic rifle, a pistol and at least one hand grenade. He eventually turned his gun on himself and was discovered by police, dead, inside the village school.

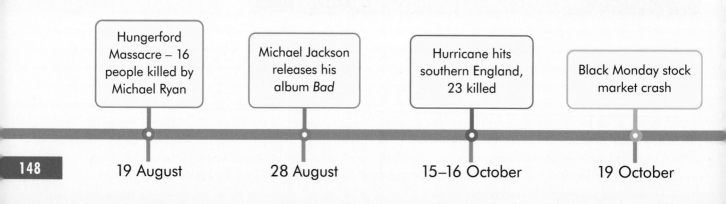

Hungerford Massacre – 16 people killed by Michael Ryan

19 August

Michael Jackson releases his album *Bad*

28 August

Hurricane hits southern England, 23 killed

15–16 October

Black Monday stock market crash

19 October

A hurricane ravaged Southern England on the night of October 16th. The Met Office was criticised for not giving warnings about its arrival.

There was a fire at King's Cross railway station in London on the night of November 18th, in which 27 people died. A carelessly dropped cigarette is believed to have set fire to a wooden escalator at about 7.30pm. Terrified passengers had to contend with a fireball that engulfed the ticket hall, filling it with dense black smoke. ITN pictures of the smoke and the rescue operation reached the studios just in time for reporters on *News at Ten* to add live commentaries to the pictures as they came in.

Above: An aerial view of Hungerford, which came into the news when Michael Ryan went on a shooting spree.

Above left and right: The hurricane that hit southern England in October 1987 caused massive damage to property across the area.

Far left and left: The aftermath of the fire at Kings Cross Station, in which 27 people died.

Fire in King's Cross underground	Reagan and Gorbachev sign INF treaty in Washington	Digging of the Channel Tunnel begins
18 November	December	1 December

Above: The nose of Pan Am *Maid of the Seas*, which blew up over Lockerbie in Scotland.

Above: A farmer surveys a large chunk of the plane that has landed in his fields. The wreckage was spread across miles.

One of Britain's worst-ever terrorist attacks took place in the skies above the Scottish town of Lockerbie on the night of December 21st. A bomb exploded on Pan Am Flight 103, which had left Heathrow at 6.25pm, bound for New York. Reports began to come in to ITN of what, at first, was thought to be a light plane crash. When the newsdesk checked out that report they were then told two RAF planes had crashed into one another.

The North of England correspondent, Mark Webster, was the nearest ITN reporter to the scene. He sped there but had trouble getting close because so many emergency vehicles were there and because his car's tyres were punctured by debris lying on the road. He managed, however, to phone in a live report to *News at Ten* using the mobile phone in the crew car. Hand-held mobiles were pretty rare at that time.

There was another terrible loss of life that year in the fire on the *Piper Alpha* North Sea oil platform. 167 workers lost their lives in two explosions about 20 minutes apart. The first was caused by a build-up of condensed natural gas beneath the platform and this in turn led to a second, even larger explosion when a gas pipeline ruptured in the heat of the fire. The situation was made worse by the fact that a second platform nearby, *Tartan*, continued to pump gas into the inferno even though those aboard could see *Piper Alpha* burning – the flames were visible for 60 miles. Apparently *Tartan's* crew lacked authorisation to shut down production. The explosions happened around 10.30pm on July 6th. Most people woke up to the news the following morning, but there would be no pictures of the disaster – or so ITN journalists thought – because the rig was so far out to sea. But, by an amazing coincidence, a documentary crew from Scottish Television had been in the area at the time. They initially wanted to keep their exclusive pictures for their own, now highly topical, story but the

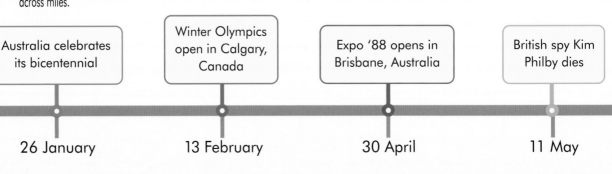

Australia celebrates its bicentennial	Winter Olympics open in Calgary, Canada	Expo '88 opens in Brisbane, Australia	British spy Kim Philby dies
26 January	13 February	30 April	11 May

pressure proved too great. By that evening's *News at 5.45*, ITN was allowed to use the pictures of the burning oil rig, which looked like something out of a disaster movie.

Above: Smoke rises from the *Piper Alpha* oil platform in the North Sea.

Alastair Stewart

Alastair Stewart was born in 1952, and studied politics, sociology and economics at Bristol University. He then became deputy president of the National Union of Students from 1974 to 1976. He worked as a reporter and presenter for Southern Television in the late seventies and joined ITN, as an industrial correspondent, in 1980. He was a presenter and reporter for *Channel 4 News* and *The Parliament Programme* before moving to *News at Ten* in 1989. After spending 1990 working as ITN's Washington correspondent he then returned to *News at Ten*. He covered the first Gulf War, live from Saudi Arabia and was the first British reporter to broadcast live from the newly-liberated Kuwait City in 1991. He has also commentated on numerous 'state occasions' and was commentating live on the Space Shuttle *Challenger* when the mission ended in disaster. He presented GMTV's *Sunday Show* and now co-presents *London Tonight* and has his own interview programme on the *ITV News Channel*. He won the Royal Television Society Presenter of the Year award in 2005.

Above: The fire took the lives of 167 men but was eventually quenched by the legendary Red Adair.

Soviet troops begin to withdraw from Afghanistan

Queen Elizabeth strips jockey Lester Piggott of his OBE after his jail sentence for tax evasion

Kylie Minogue releases her debut album, *Kylie*

15 May

6 June

July

Right: The Royal family tries to put across the image of a big, happy family during a photocall at Sandringham.

Above: At least two of the younger members were genuinely happy.

To those who knew, the signs were there. The marriage of the Prince and Princess of Wales was in trouble, but they kept up appearances, especially with their young sons. And they kept up their public duties with a royal tour of Australia. ITN broadcast a special programme of their visit which was part of Australia's bicentennial celebrations. In the year that Prince Charles turned 40 he came worryingly close to losing his life when an avalanche struck the royal party as they skied off-piste in Klosters, killing his friend, Major Hugh Lindsay. When reports of the accident first reached ITN it seemed that Prince Charles himself might have been killed. In fact the Prince – who was leading the group – had managed to ski to safety along with the rest of the party. Once the danger had passed, Charles and the others raced back to the scene and dug with their hands to try to reach Major Lindsay. The Prince took his death badly; not only

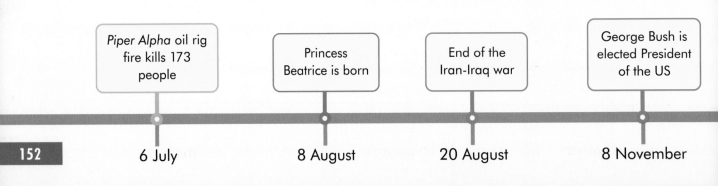

Piper Alpha oil rig fire kills 173 people	Princess Beatrice is born	End of the Iran-Iraq war	George Bush is elected President of the US
6 July	8 August	20 August	8 November

had he been a close friend, but Charles blamed himself, as leader of the party, for what had happened.

At the end of the year another rail disaster occurred when three trains were involved in a collision at Clapham in South London, during the morning rush hour on December 12th. Firemen had to cut survivors from the mangled wreckage as doctors performed surgery on site in a desperate attempt to save lives. The final death toll was 35 and the accident was blamed on a faulty signal, installed during an upgrade to the local signalling network. There were ITN newsflashes throughout the morning as more details and more pictures came through. It later became clear that one driver had stopped his train at the faulty signal but nothing alerted the second driver that there was a train on the line ahead. The second train ran into the back of the first and a third, empty, train later ran into the wreckage, killing some passengers who had survived the first crash.

Above left and right: Princess Diana was looking less and less happy as she carried out her public duties with her husband.

Clapham rail crash – 35 killed and 132 injured

Rain Man, starring Dustin Hoffman and Tom Cruise, is released

PanAm airliner *Maid of the Seas* is blown up over Lockerbie in Scotland

12 December

16 December

21 December

Above left, middle and right: The aftermath of the violence in Tiananmen Square in Beijing. Students congregate in silence, a young girl weeps as she speaks of what happened, and the bodies of students are laid out for formal identification.

Above: Floral tributes are left at the gates of the Hillsborough Stadium.

For seven weeks, ITN had been reporting the growing pro-democracy campaign in the Chinese capital Beijing. Peaceful rallies had been held in the city's Tiananmen Square, but the protests were brought to a very abrupt and brutal end when tanks were sent to clear the demonstrators from the square. The protest, in support of democratic reform and against government corruption, was timed to coincide with the visit to China of Soviet President Mikhail Gorbachev. On May 4th, over 100,000 people had marched through the capital. A huge statue, modelled on New York's Statue of Liberty, was set up in front of the Great Hall of the People and became the symbol of the students' protest to TV viewers around the world. The Chinese authorities believed that the situation was in imminent danger of escalating beyond their control, so they decided to send in the troops. This resulted in one of the defining images of the decade: a lone figure, carrying shopping bags, confronting and halting a column of tanks for over half an hour.

But it proved to be just a delay and elements of the Chinese 27th Army duly advanced. At first the troops fired over the protesters' heads, but then lowered their aim. Fatalities, according to the Chinese Red Cross, totalled over 2,500 – some estimates put the figure far higher. The number of injured may have

Kegworth Air Disaster – Boeing 737 crashes on approach to East Midlands Airport, 44 killed

Ayatollah Khomeini declares a fatwa against Salman Rushdie

Last Soviet troops leave Afghanistan

8 January

14 Febraury

14 February

exceeded 10,000. The brutality of the action caused widespread international condemnation, largely due to the graphic images, relayed across the globe, of events that once would have been kept very secret indeed.

After 10 years of occupation, the Soviet Union pulled its troops out of Afghanistan. Some 15,000 Russian soldiers had died in the conflict, along with countless Afghans. It was a humiliating climb-down for the tanks of a superpower to be defeated by Mujahideen fighters, who often used horses to get around. Newscaster Sandy Gall left the relative comfort of the studio to join ITN's reporting team on the withdrawal. Among his equipment was a satellite dish that could be collapsed into pieces, packed into boxes and transported by two or three horses. Sandy's remarkable reports gave viewers a real understanding of what it was like to be with the Mujahideen, trekking through the mountains as the Soviet Union withdrew.

Meanwhile, Jon Snow was giving up his job as ITN's Diplomatic Editor on *ITV News* to take up permanent newscasting as the new presenter of *Channel 4 News*. He took over from Peter Sissons, who was leaving for the BBC.

Above left, middle and right: Russian occupation of Afghanistan is brought to an end and soldiers prepare to leave for home. There had been thousands of casualties on both sides, and the country was left in chaos.

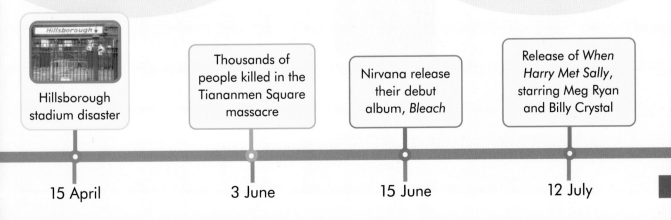

Hillsborough stadium disaster

Thousands of people killed in the Tiananmen Square massacre

Nirvana release their debut album, *Bleach*

Release of *When Harry Met Sally*, starring Meg Ryan and Billy Crystal

15 April

3 June

15 June

12 July

155

Above: Ian Glover-James reports to camera.

In a strange twist of fate, ITN's Moscow Correspondent, Ian Glover-James, found himself reporting on his own expulsion from the Soviet Union, in a diplomatic row between Russia and Britain. The British Government had ordered the expulsion of 11 Soviet diplomats and journalists for spying. In retaliation, out went Ian, two other British journalists and eight diplomats.

The big story of the year was, without a doubt, the fall of the Berlin Wall in November. It had stood for more than quarter of a century – dividing Germany, East from West. ITN had been reporting the pressure on East Germany's communist leader, Eric Honecker. He had refused to listen either to his own people or even to the Soviet leader, Mikhail Gorbachev, on the need to give them more freedom. In the end, Honecker was thrown out by his own Communist Party. When the announcement came that the gates and checkpoints along the wall were to be opened, East Berliners could

Marchioness Disaster – 51 die when a pleasure boat collides with a barge on the Thames

Princess Diana's brother, Earl Spencer, marries at Althorp

Earthquake in San Francisco kills 63

Guildford Four released

20 August

16 September

17 October

19 October

hardly believe it. As they streamed out into West Germany, ITN reporters poured in to cover the amazing scenes in a series of live programmes.

But the collapse of the old Soviet bloc did not end there – the people of Romania then staged their revolution. ITN reporters Paul Davies and Colin Baker were despatched, separately, to Romania. Paul chartered a small plane to get into Bucharest airport but the ITN team were told they couldn't land because of the fighting. It was only when the pilot pretended to air traffic control that he was running low on fuel that they were allowed down. As their plane had been diverted, Colin Baker headed to the town of Timisoara, where the revolution had begun, by vehicle convoy, with the letters 'TV' on the side of their vans written in masking tape. It was a frightening journey. When they arrived, they found the lorry carrying the satellite dish had bullet holes in it but fortunately none of those inside, or the equipment, had been hit. Christmas, normally a quiet time for news, was dominated by the overthrow and execution of the Romanian dictator, Nicolae Ceausescu and ITN teams were there to see history made.

Above from left to right: After people in West Berlin attack the Berlin Wall with sledgehammers, a large section collapses to loud cheers. East German guards, seen through the gap, smile at the crowds on the other side.

Demolition of the Berlin Wall begins

Born on the Fourth of July, starring Tom Cruise, is released

Nicolae Ceausescu, dictator of Romania, is executed

10 November

20 December

25 December

1990s

The 1990s provided ITN with some of its greatest world exclusives, among them the first interview with the released ANC leader Nelson Mandela and the discovery of Serbian-run detention camps in Bosnia where Muslim men were held in terrible conditions. By the end of the decade *News at Ten* finally ended its run, 32 years after starting out as a 13 week experiment, but new ITN programmes took their places in the ITV schedules.

Top: Workers cutting meat in a warehouse in Europe, seen through two hanging carcasses in foreground.

Above: Agriculture Minister John Selwyn Gummer offers his young daughter a beef burger during the height of the Mad Cow disease scare.

Above: Former Prime Minister Margaret Thatcher leaves 10 Downing Street for the last time with her husband Denis Thatcher.

With Britain in the grip of 'mad cow' disease or BSE, Agriculture Minister John Gummer was determined to prove British beef was safe to eat. In front of the cameras, at a local show in Ipswich, he took a large bite out of a burger. When that didn't appear to impress watching reporters, he handed the burger to his young daughter. The gesture, shown by ITN, had a touch of desperation about it, reflecting the anxieties in Government.

BSE was first identified in 1986, but had reached worrying levels. Its origin is disputed but its spread was increased by meat and bone meal from infected animals being fed to healthy herds. The human form, variant Creutzfeldt-Jakob Disease, has proved rare despite fears of an epidemic, but in a report in 2001, 88 of the 92 recorded cases were in the UK. Shoppers stopped buying British beef, hospitals and schools dropped it from their menus and other countries blocked imports. ITN reported the science around the spread of the disease and the impact on the meat and livestock industries.

Mrs Thatcher's uncompromising style of government, so admired during the Falklands campaign, finally took its toll. On November 22nd ITN broke into programmes to carry pictures of her leaving Downing Street for the last time, with a hint of a tear in her eye. Perhaps the final straw had been her decision, against the advice of many in her own ranks, to introduce the community charge, unpopularly known as the poll tax, to replace the old rates system. It became the cause of some of the worst rioting in London – ITN's live reports showed a pall of smoke over Trafalgar Square, beneath which protesters fought pitched battles with police. After Mrs Thatcher's resignation she was replaced by John Major who, earlier in the year, as Chancellor of the Exchequer, had presented the first televised budget.

ITN's big coup of the year was Nelson Mandela's first TV interview after his release, when Trevor McDonald spoke to the ANC leader in the garden of his home in Soweto. ITN scooped the interview after offering to draw up a

The first McDonald's opens in Moscow

Nelson Mandela released

Brixton is sealed off after a night of Poll Tax riots

Mikhail Gorbachev is elected as the first executive president of the Soviet Union

31 January   11 February   9 March   15 March

media plan to help the trades union organisation deal with the massive interest from journalists around the world.

Meanwhile back in London, ITN had outgrown its base in Wells Street and a new, purpose-built HQ, designed by Sir Norman Foster, was built in Gray's Inn Road in London. For a time programmes were broadcast from two different buildings, while the change over was completed.

Julia Somerville

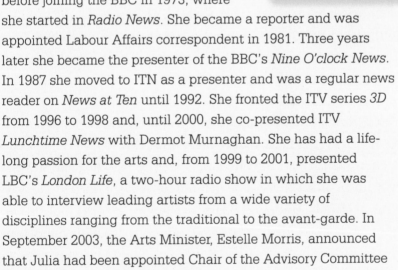

Julia Somerville joined IPC Media on graduating from the University of Sussex. She worked on *Homes and Gardens*, *Woman's Journal* and *Woman's Own* before joining the BBC in 1973, where she started in *Radio News*. She became a reporter and was appointed Labour Affairs correspondent in 1981. Three years later she became the presenter of the BBC's *Nine O'clock News*. In 1987 she moved to ITN as a presenter and was a regular news reader on *News at Ten* until 1992. She fronted the ITV series *3D* from 1996 to 1998 and, until 2000, she co-presented ITV *Lunchtime News* with Dermot Murnaghan. She has had a life-long passion for the arts and, from 1999 to 2001, presented LBC's *London Life*, a two-hour radio show in which she was able to interview leading artists from a wide variety of disciplines ranging from the traditional to the avant-garde. In September 2003, the Arts Minister, Estelle Morris, announced that Julia had been appointed Chair of the Advisory Committee of the Government Art Collection.

Above: The front of the Anti-Poll Tax march clashed violently with police officers and both marchers and police were injured.

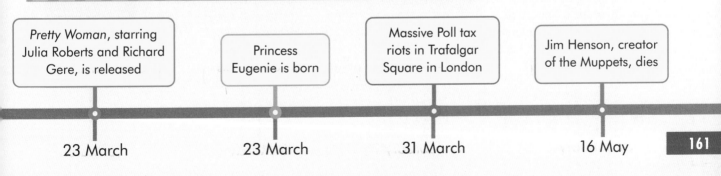

Pretty Woman, starring Julia Roberts and Richard Gere, is released

Princess Eugenie is born

Massive Poll tax riots in Trafalgar Square in London

Jim Henson, creator of the Muppets, dies

23 March

23 March

31 March

16 May

Above left: Defiant Iraqi President Saddam Hussein inspects his troops soon after their arrival in Kuwait.

Above right: Iraqi troops cheer their leader.

Above: Nelson Mandela speaks to supporters after his release from 27 years imprisonment in South Africa.

On a quiet August weekend, reports reached the ITN newsroom that Iraqi troops had invaded Kuwait. Iraqi tanks and troops rolled across the border and were soon in control of the capital Kuwait City. ITN staff were scrambled as shaky pictures were said to be on their way. It was the start of the build up to the first Gulf War.

The Iraqi president, Saddam Hussein, claimed Kuwait had stolen oil from a disputed field and he was also angry that Kuwait had increased its oil production, which had the effect of lowering prices. That, in turn, had affected Iraq's oil revenues. The invasion of Kuwait opened the way to an invasion of Saudi Arabia. Saddam strenuously denied that this was his intention, whilst moving his armoured divisions up to the Saudi border.

Agriculture Minister John Gummer feeds a hamburger to his 5-year-old daughter to counter rumours about Mad Cow Disease (BSE)

Hubble Space Telescope becomes operative

Mariah Carey releases her debut album, *Mariah Carey*

Major earthquake in Iran

19 May

20 May

12 June

21 June

America issued an ultimatum to Saddam to pull out of Kuwait. When he refused, American and British troops began arriving in the Gulf, primarily in Saudi Arabia, and ITN teams went with them. They attached themselves to RAF, Navy, and Army units. The term 'embedded' was still to become common, but most of them lived and dressed as soldiers while reporting the war. Technology had moved on from the last big conflict, the Falklands. Satellite dishes were far more portable and military officials realised they wouldn't be able to control the flow of information in the way they had done more than a decade earlier.

While ITN staff were waiting in the Gulf, another waiting game was going on under the English Channel. On December 1st, British and French engineers achieved the first historic breakthrough in the Channel tunnel that would link Britain and France. ITN produced a special programme, with pictures from inside the tunnel, of the famous handshake beneath the sea.

Above top and bottom: Ruined buildings in the remote village of Khalesham after an earthquake devastated the Zanjun Province of Iran.

Left: ITN reporter Robert Moore reports from the scene as rescue workers bring aid to those still alive. Refugees were housed in a city of tents.

Channel Tunnel workers from England and France meet under the Channel

Iraq invades Kuwait, leading to the Gulf War

East Germany becomes part of Germany again

Margaret Thatcher resigns – John Major becomes Prime Minister on 22 November

2 August

3 October

22 November

1 December

1991 War

Above: General Schwarzkopf, commander of US troops during the Gulf War.

Above: US Marines loading and firing Howitzer guns during the battle for Al Khafji in the Gulf War.

Right: The Baghdad skyline at night, lit up with anti-aircraft tracer fire in search of attacking allied jets.

The Gulf war, when it came, was a frightening time for ITN staff in the Gulf. The United States and its allies had given Saddam Hussein until January 15th to pull his troops out of Kuwait. He didn't and the war began the following day. The first inkling at ITN was while Middle East correspondent Brent Sadler was talking to London on a special CNN sound circuit. Suddenly CNN asked if they could have it back – the bombing of Baghdad had started. ITN broke into *Midweek Sports Special* at 11.47pm and kept going for seven hours.

ITN took the difficult decision to keep Brent Sadler and his crew in Baghdad during the war as bombs and missiles fell on targets in the city – as not all were accurate. The decision was rewarded with one of the most remarkable images of the war – the sight of American missiles flying low overhead towards their targets. As Brent described in a memorable piece to camera, they were 'map-reading themselves' along Iraqi motorways.

ITN cameraman Eugene Campbell had several dangerous assignments in the Gulf. While on board *HMS Gloucester* he got on well with the ship's Lynx helicopter crews and was eventually invited along on one of their search and destroy missions. The day had begun as normal with breakfast. The next meal was handed to them as they prepared to climb aboard the helicopter... packed lunches in brown paper bags. They flew along the Kuwaiti coastline – about a mile and a half out to sea and supposedly out of range of the Iraqi surface to air missiles. They came across an Iraqi warship and the pilot requested permission from the American command ship to fire one of its Sea Skua missiles at the Iraqi vessel. Once permission was granted, the helicopter had to hover while its

Coalition forces drive Iraqi troops out of Kuwait

IRA fires a mortar bomb into the garden behind 10 Downing Street

Release of *The Silence of the Lambs*, starring Anthony Hopkins and Jodie Foster

Operation Desert Storm begins in Kuwait

February   7 February   13 February   24 February

Far left: Local Kuwaitis celebrate as liberating armoured columns of allied troops parade through the city centre.

Left: A defaced portrait of Iraqi leader Saddam Hussein is burned by the freed city dwellers.

radar locked onto the target, continuing to hover even after the missile was on its way, to make sure it had the right coordinates. For a few terrifying moments the helicopter was a sitting target for the Iraqi warship's anti-aircraft guns. The ship was hit and almost certainly sank. It was a highly charged moment and a shocking experience, and marked an improbably stark contrast with what happened next. As they flew back to *HMS Gloucester*, the helicopter pilot, navigator and Eugene opened their brown paper parcels and ate their lunch of cheese and crackers.

Above: A seabird completely covered in oil struggles in an oily sea.

There were many television firsts in ITN's coverage of the war, one of which was Alastair Stewart presenting *News at Ten* live from Kuwait on the day of liberation by Saudi forces. Alastair had travelled with the Saudis as they crossed the border into Kuwait. They were welcomed by delighted Kuwaitis who almost swamped Alastair as he made his live broadcasts.

One other reporter not with British forces was Peter Sharp – he was in the city of Khafji on Kuwait's border with Saudi Arabia. One day the smell of petrol or diesel fumes filled the air, which he assumed was from the camera crew's generator – until he saw a cormorant covered in oil. He was the first person to realise that Iraq had attacked Kuwait's oil installations and left them pouring thousands of gallons of crude oil into the sea. It was an ecological disaster that no one had anticipated and he and his crew worked into the night to compile a report. The next day they woke to see President Bush Senior on CNN talking about the pictures they had sent in.

Above: ITN featured an exclusive report on the devastating impact on the environmental of the crude oil dumped by Iraqis into the sea.

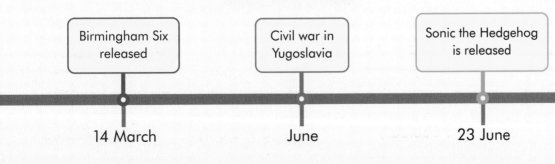

Birmingham Six released	Civil war in Yugoslavia	Sonic the Hedgehog is released
14 March	June	23 June

Far right: Terry Waite, the British hostage released from captivity in Beirut, returns back home to Britain on an RAF plane.

Below left: ITN had the only Western reporter on the ground during the Siege of Dubrovnik. Paul Davies filed exclusive reports as shells exploded around him, destroying buildings and setting the city ablaze. Historic buildings, some over 400 years old, were destroyed during the bombardment. Civilians left in the city ran for cover, or tried to rescue their possessions.

Below right: A general view of the old city with black smoke rising as incoming shells strike home.

There was an emotional return to Britain for Terry Waite, the man who went to Beirut to try to free foreign hostages, including Briton John McCarthy, and ended up becoming one himself. ITN was at RAF Lyneham for his return. He had left Britain almost five years earlier, as the special envoy of the Archbishop of Canterbury, and managed to secure a meeting with the kidnap group Islamic Jihad but was then captured himself.

He remained in captivity for almost five years and spent much of that time manacled, in solitary confinement, in a windowless cellar. He was released on November 18th, together with an American hostage, Tom Sutherland, and returned to England the following day. The hostages whose release he had sought to secure were all freed within six months.

The Soviet Union begins to collapse as Estonia, Latvia, Ukraine, Kyrgystan and Uzbekistan all declare their independence within a few days

Journalist John McCarthy is released from captivity in Lebanon

Nirvana release their album *Nevermind*

August

8 August

24 September

Inset: Soviet President Mikhail Gorbachev after the coup, as Yeltsin calls for suspension of Russian Communist Party.

Left: Makeshift barricades and wreckage across the road in front of the Russian House of Soviets – the 'White House' – which Russian Federation President Boris Yeltsin was holding in coup.

Above: William Kennedy Smith in court in Palm Beach, Florida, facing a charge of rape.

In Croatia, at the centre of another vicious, ethnic conflict, ITN reporter David Chater was shot in the back by a sniper in the ruined city of Vukovar. Michael Nicholson, reporting from the same city, told the story of a baby girl, born during the bombardment, who had been horribly injured by shrapnel. Little Sanja became a symbol of war's cruelty and futility – and survived.

However, Mikhail Gorbachev did not survive as Soviet President. He had managed to hold on to power despite a coup staged by a group of hardline plotters opposed to his reforming views. But as the Soviet Union started to disintegrate, he decided he could no longer stay in office.

Above: Imelda Marcos, wife of deceased ex President Ferdinand, returns to rapturous welcome in the Philippines.

Siege of Dubrovnik

Robert Maxwell falls off his yacht and drowns

Terry Waite and fellow hostage American Tom Sutherland are released

Freddie Mercury, lead singer of Queen, dies

November

5 November

18 November

24 November

1992 Balkan Conflict

Above: An ITN Exclusive report into the Serbian-run Omarska and Trnopolje prisoner of war camps in Bosnia, revealed that emaciated Muslim prisoners were being held in conditions of near-starvation. ITN reporters Ian Williams and Penny Marshall, below, were denied access to the accommodation block at the camp by an interpreter Nana Balban, speaking on behalf of the Camp Commandant. The Commandant assured them that the camp was only a transit centre and that no prisoners were held there long term.

ITN's Penny Marshall and Ian Williams brought home the horror of the conflict in Bosnia with exclusive reports from a Serb-run detention camp where Muslim men were being held in shocking conditions. The scenes were terrifyingly reminiscent of images of the Nazi concentration camps of the Second World War – the men were starved and emaciated and kept behind barbed wire. Penny's report occupied the whole of the first half of that night's *News at Ten*, Ian's led *Channel 4 News*. Their pictures covered the front pages of the following day's newspapers across the world. It was probably no coincidence that military intervention in Bosnia by the Western powers followed swiftly.

ITN reporter Michael Nicholson had been visiting orphanages in Sarajevo, where the conditions were little better. Aid workers were struggling to cope with great numbers of orphaned and abandoned children. Their plight was pitiful and Nicholson implored viewers to try to help in whatever way they could. The British public rose to the challenge and a massive relief effort was quickly under way. For his own part, Michael Nicholson took on the challenge by rescuing a young girl called Natasha, eventually managing to adopt her. He later published a book about this remarkable episode, *Natasha's Story*, and this was subsequently adapted for the screen. The film, *Welcome to Sarajevo*, was directed by Michael Winterbottom, with Stephen Dillane playing the part of 'Michael Henderson' and included actual ITN footage. It was released in 1997.

The Socialist Federal Republic of Yugoslavia ceases to exist and Slovenia and Croatia gain independence

Boxer Mike Tyson is convicted of rape

Art band The KLF cause havoc at the Brit Awards

Civil war breaks out in Bosnia

15 January   10 February   11 February   March

Julian Manyon

Julian Manyon's career as a journalist began in the late 1960s when he worked as a freelance reporter in Vietnam and Cambodia. By the end of the war he was reporting for Independent Radio News and had published a book entitled *The Fall of Saigon*. He subsequently worked on BBC Radio 4's *World at One* before moving to BBC TV's *Tonight* programme. He joined Thames TV in 1978 and made over 90 films for *This Week* and *TV Eye*. During the Falklands War he was taken prisoner by the Argentinian secret police but secured the only interview with General Galtieri. He was also the reporter on the highly controversial *Death on the Rock* documentary that detailed the tracking and killing of three IRA members by British special forces on Gibraltar in 1988. The programme caused great consternation to Mrs Thatcher's government and attempts were made to prevent its being broadcast. They failed and *Death on the Rock* won a BAFTA award. Julian joined ITN in 1992 and has distinguished himself with award-winning coverage from Moscow, Chechnya, Belgrade and during the 2003 Gulf War. In 2004 he scooped the world with his reporting of the Beslan school siege, winning a Gold Nymph at the Monte Carlo Awards in 2005 for his courageous and gripping coverage of this event. He is now ITV News' Middle East correspondent.

Above: A line of emaciated Muslim prisoners standing behind a wire fence at Trnopolje camp. The prisoners lived in an open field in the intense heat.

Above: Prisoners are afraid to talk to the camera, but some say that they have seen others being beaten, and that men have disappeared.

Above: Emaciated prisoner Fikret Alic, with the bones of his ribcage protruding clearly, standing behind a barbed wire fence.

Duke and Duchess of York announce they are to separate

The Princess Royal divorces her husband, Captain Mark Philips

John Major is re-elected as Prime Minister

19 March

April

9 April

As polling day approached in the 1992 General Election, it seemed to many that it was going to go Labour's way. Certainly the Labour leader Neil Kinnock seemed to think so at an eve of election rally in Sheffield, as anyone watching *News at Ten* that night would have seen. He and most of his shadow cabinet took to the stage and acted as if it were in the bag.

But John Major, thought of as the grey man of British politics, had a surprise for them. He had been selected by the Conservative Party to replace Margaret Thatcher as Prime Minister two years previously and now went to the country to seek their approval for a fourth term in office for the Tories. Major was not highly regarded by many political commentators but, during his short residency at Number 10, he had already had to cope with Britain's involvement in the Gulf War, the removal of the despised poll tax that had been Mrs Thatcher's undoing, and the final negotiation of the Maastricht Treaty which led to the creation of the single European currency – the Euro. ITN had covered his campaign, much of which was conducted from an old fashioned soap box. It was undoubtedly a gimmick but his approach seemed to work. Mr Major was returned with an overall majority of 21 seats and Neil Kinnock, having now been defeated twice as Labour leader, resigned soon afterwards.

Top: Fire raging at Windsor Castle – smoke pours out of the building as fire fighters try to stem the terrible blaze.

Above: During a speech in London, Queen Elizabeth II tells listeners that 1992 has been an *'annus horibilis'*.

EuroDisney opens in France

Comedian Benny Hill dies

Race riots in Los Angeles after acquittal of police accused of beating a black motorist

12 April

18 April

29 April

Within months, Mr Major's new Government was in deep trouble. The pound had been sliding below its accepted level in the European Exchange Rate Mechanism. The Bank of England had tried to prop up its value by buying sterling, but it wasn't enough. Despite two interest rate rises in one day, Mr Major and his Chancellor, Norman Lamont, took the decision to pull Britain out of the Exchange Rate Mechanism – effectively devaluing the pound. A flustered Mr Lamont emerged from the Treasury to make the announcement while *Channel 4 News* was on air. The programme's viewers that night were the first to know what had happened.

Mr Lamont wasn't the only person in public life having a difficult time – the Queen talked openly about the unhappy events of the previous months. As ITN viewers heard, the Queen was suffering from a sore throat at a dinner at London's Guildhall, which seemed to confirm what a miserable year she'd had. '1992 is not,' she said in a croaky voice, 'a year I shall look back on with undiluted pleasure. In the words of one of my more sympathetic correspondents, it has turned out to be an "*annus horribilis*"'.

The revelations about the state of the Prince and Princess of Wales' marriage, by author Andrew Morton, had contributed to the Queen's bad year. Viewers who had seen ITN pictures of the royal couple's awkward body language on their trip to South Korea suddenly understood. Their separation was officially announced in December. And shortly before the Queen gave her speech, Windsor Castle had caught fire. ITN camera teams rushed to the scene and were in time to film the smoke still engulfing some of the state apartments and to talk to Prince Andrew who had organised a human chain of staff to pass valuable paintings out of harm's way.

Above: Princess Diana fights back tears during a visit to a hospice in Southport, following publication of allegations that she had attempted suicide in the past.

Above: The Royal couple look strained during their official visit to South Korea.

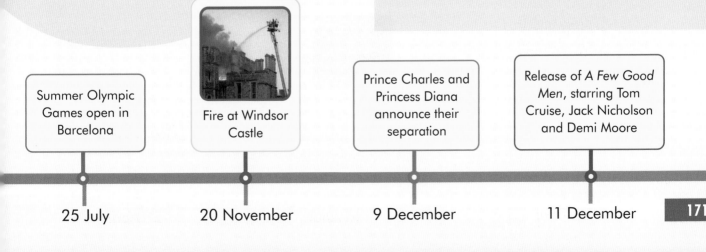

Summer Olympic Games open in Barcelona	Fire at Windsor Castle	Prince Charles and Princess Diana announce their separation	Release of *A Few Good Men*, starring Tom Cruise, Jack Nicholson and Demi Moore
25 July	20 November	9 December	11 December

Right: Ceremonial soldiers march outside as Buckingham Palace opens to paying visitors for the very first time.

Far right: Princess Diana speaks about needing time and space, signalling her partial withdrawal from public life. She says that she finds the constant attention overwhelming, affecting both her public duties and her private life, and that she intends to spend more time with her sons.

Above: Camilla Parker Bowles at a polo match. She was a close friend of the Prince of Wales even before his marriage to Diana.

ITN cameras were invited into Buckingham Palace for a preview of its opening to the public for the first time. The idea was to allow paying visitors to see some of the state rooms while the Queen and Prince Philip were on holiday in July and August. The money raised went to pay for the repair and restoration of those parts of Windsor Castle damaged by the fire at the end of the previous year. ITN was back to film the queues for tickets when the Palace gates opened.

The public, however, were given glimpses into the private lives of Prince Charles and Princess Diana that Buckingham Palace would rather they had not seen. Two newspapers printed details of an intimate telephone conversation said to be between the Prince and Camilla Parker Bowles, which had apparently been recorded by amateur radio operators – although some suspected that rogue elements in British intelligence were involved. ITN brought in voice coaches to assess whether it really was Prince Charles and Camilla. One newspaper also printed photographs of Princess Diana working out at a London gym in her singlet and lycra shorts. In an unusual

Czechoslovakia divides into Slovakia and Czech Republic

Bill Clinton inaugurated as President of the US

Groundhog Day, starring Bill Murray and Andie MacDowell, is released

1 January

20 January

12 February

Above: The devastated town centre of Portadown, following the explosion of a massive IRA terrorist bomb.

Above: Emergency services at the scene of the attack. Superintendent Jimmy Blair (RUC) tells ITN reporter Andrew Simmons that police action prevented many casualties.

decision for a member of the royal family, the Princess issued a writ against Mirror Group Newspapers and the owner of the gym who had taken the photographs.

In October, in a Belfast street crowded with shoppers, two members of the Provisional IRA walked into a fish and chip shop and set off a bomb that killed nine people – and one of the bombers. It happened in the Protestant stronghold of the Shankhill Road and the target was the upstairs meeting room of the outlawed Ulster Defence Association. It very nearly triggered a full scale civil war. There were also IRA bombings at Bishopsgate in the City of London where three people died, and in Warrington where two young boys, Tim Parry and Jonathan Ball, were killed.

Above: ITN had exclusive footage of an IRA lorry bomb exploding in the City of London. The street after the explosion was a scene of devastation, with debris everywhere.

Toddler James Bulger is murdered by two older children

Footballer Bobby Moore dies

A bomb goes off next to the North Tower of the World Trade Center, killing six and injuring 1,000

Waco Siege begins in Texas, when US Bureau of Alcohol, Tobacco and Firearms attempt to arrest cult leader David Koresh

12 February   24 February   26 February   28 February

Above: Democratic candidate Bill Clinton is elected President of the United States.

Below left: Residents of Iowa take to boats to get around, as rain continues to pour down. Some have lost everything in the floods.

Below right: A general view of the flooded business district of Des Moines, in Iowa. Whole areas were completely underwater, with only house rooftops showing.

When Bill Clinton took over as 42nd President of the United States, little can have prepared him for the series of catastrophes in the year ahead. The United States suffered the worst floods of the 20th century and the Mississippi Basin was swamped, as was much of the Mid West, causing 50 deaths and damage costing some US$20 billion. 10,000 homes were totally destroyed.

A bomb was planted at the World Trade Center in New York; six people were killed and over 1,000 injured. Osama Bin Laden denied responsibility but praised the attack. Under pressure from the US government and the Saudis, Bin Laden was forced to transfer his headquarters from Sudan to Afghanistan.

18 American servicemen were killed when their aircraft was shot down over Mogadishu in Somalia and their bodies dragged through the streets. Two years later Osama Bin Laden was indicted in his absence for training the guerrillas involved in the attack.

Great Blizzard leads to snowstorms and floods across North America from Cuba to Quebec

13 March

IRA bomb explodes in Warrington Town Centre, killing two children

20 March

Bomb explodes in Bishopsgate, killing 1 and injuring 50

24 April

Buckingham Palace is opened to the public for the first time

7 August

A town in Texas called Waco became the centre of the world's attention for 51 days in a siege that ended in terrible bloodshed. An ITN team joined the international media camp that sprang up there. Local police believed members of the Branch Davidian Cult had been stockpiling weapons at their home, and they staged a raid in which four police officers were shot. The cult members, followers of a man called David Koresh, then barricaded themselves in.

When the police finally stormed the building, the cult members inside set fire to it and themselves in a final and fatal act of defiance. When it was all over, the bodies of David Koresh and 66 of his followers were found inside.

ITN's coverage of the Waco seige on *News at Ten* pioneered the use of three-dimensional computer graphics to give viewers a truly visual understanding of the events taking place, the first broadcast ever to do so.

Above left: Investigators and police search the smoking remains of the Branch Davidians' ranch at Mount Carmel near Waco after the apparent mass suicide of the inmates by fire. The FBI insisted that the fire was started on the inside.

Above right: Survivors, in orange prison clothing, tell reporters that they did not start the fire.

There was a different kind of siege in Russia. ITN reporter Julian Manyon and his crew filmed incredible scenes of the siege of the Russian Parliament – the other White House, as it was known. President Yeltsin put down an attempt by left-wing members of the parliament to depose him by barricading them inside the building. ITN cameras filmed from close quarters as tanks of the Russian army, which had responded to his order to attack, shelled the parliament building. The battle for control lasted a day. In the end, those rebels who had survived the onslaught came out waving white flags.

Above: Police outside the school in Neuilly-sur-Seine, Paris, where gunman Eric Schmitt held children hostage in May, 1993.

Ace of Base release their album *Happy Nation US Version* (*The Sign* in the US), which becomes the highest-selling debut album of all time

An earthquake in India kills nearly 10,000

Sunday opening hours introduced

25 September

29 September

9 December

Above: In the aftermath of the Rwandan massacre, the inhabitants of Nyatama walk along the road back to their homes carrying their few possessions.

J ulian Manyon, who had reported on the attempted coup in Moscow the previous year, was sent to Bukavu on the border between Zaire and Rwanda where rival tribes, the Tutsis and Hutus, were fighting for supremacy. The scale of the killing was first indicated by the tens of thousands of refugees fleeing across the border into Zaire, but the appalling level of brutality was only revealed by the mounds of corpses. 100,000 Tutsis had been massacred by Hutu soldiers. Julian Manyon's revelation of the Rwandan genocide won a Royal Television Society award.

Far better news was reported from South Africa where, for the first time, preparations were in progress for the country's first non-racial elections. ITN filmed from the ground and from the air as people queued in their thousands to vote. Polling stations had to stay open into the night to cope with the huge turn out of people, who had waited so long to take part in elections for the first time in their lives. Nelson Mandela, who had been imprisoned for 27 years, led his party, the African National Congress, which had been banned for 30 years, to victory by winning 62 per cent of

Right: A human skull lying on ground among clothes – the bodies are still lying where they fell.

Far right: A young girl with a bandaged face. One 12-year-old child spent seven days hiding amongst the dead bodies in the church.

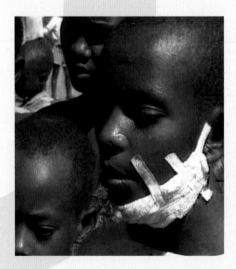

An earthquake hits San Fernando Valley in California

BMW purchases Rover from British Aerospace

Fred West arrested and charged with Cromwell Street murders

Nine Inch Nails release their album *The Downward Spiral*

17 January

31 January

28 February

8 March

the vote. By so doing, Mandela became the first democratically elected leader in South Africa's history. He was inaugurated on May 10th, at the Union Buildings in Pretoria. In his address, Mandela used the term 'national reconciliation' and this process was to become a cornerstone of the new administration.

Above: Nelson Mandela (leader of ANC) places his vote in the ballot box in the first free elections for both whites and blacks in South Africa.

Penny Marshall

Penny Marshall studied history at the London School of Economics before working at *The Listener* magazine as a sub editor and then as a reporter for the *Wimbledon News*. She joined ITN as a trainee in 1985 and became a reporter in 1989. That year Penny led the first news team to arrive in Timisoira, where the Romanian revolution began. In the summer of 1992, Penny and *Channel 4 News* correspondent Ian Williams were the first television journalists to uncover the Serb-run detention camps in Bosnia. Their subsequent reports and pictures, shown throughout the world, generated an international outcry. Penny's report won the International News Award for 1992 from the Royal Television Society. She and Ian also won the joint top prize in BAFTA's News and Actuality category and an international Emmy in the United States. Penny was appointed ITN's Defence and Diplomatic correspondent in 1995 and later become International correspondent.

Above: Thousands of township people queue in the light of early morning to cast their votes in the election. Some tell reporters that people have died for this day.

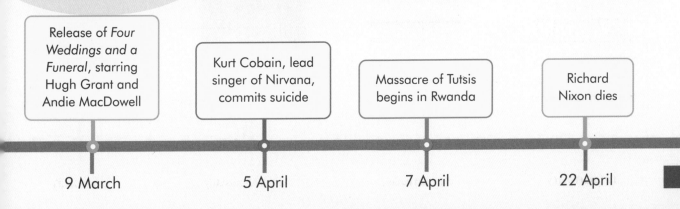

Release of *Four Weddings and a Funeral*, starring Hugh Grant and Andie MacDowell

Kurt Cobain, lead singer of Nirvana, commits suicide

Massacre of Tutsis begins in Rwanda

Richard Nixon dies

9 March

5 April

7 April

22 April

1994 Overseas News

Above left, middle and right: ITN reporter Bill Neely demonstrates the effect of the earthquake in California on the local freeway system. Many roads now have to be demolished and rebuilt.

Above: A child sleeps on the floor of a Hollywood high school gym – many families are now homeless.

At 4.31am on January 17th, an earthquake measuring 6.6 on the Richter Scale struck Northridge in Southern California. 57 people were killed and the cost of the damage was put at US$15 billion. Among the bizarre and terrifying images captured on camera were four foot 'waves' in tarmac roads and houses with collapsed walls revealing undamaged glass and china.

From Washington in September came the bizarre and alarming story of the fatal crash landing of a light aircraft in the grounds of the White House. The pilot, Frank Eugene Corder, had spent the previous evening drinking and smoking crack cocaine and was driven to Aldino Airport at Churchville, Maryland, by his brother. Just before 2pm he started the motor of a Cessna P150 light aircraft. Corder had taken lessons in the plane but was not a licensed pilot. He was picked up by Federal Aviation Authority radar just after 1am the following morning – no one knows what he was doing in the intervening 11 hours. At about 1.45am, he entered

South Africa holds its first multi-racial elections

Channel Tunnel opens

Nelson Mandela is inaugurated as President of South Africa

50th Anniversary of D-Day

26 April

6 May

9 May

6 June

restricted airspace above Washington DC and flew low towards the White House, crashing onto the lawn at 1.50 am, where he died of multiple injuries. The President and the First Lady were not at home at the time, but the incident raised serious questions about the vulnerability of the White House to attack from the air.

The Russian republic of Chechnya had become a thorn in the side of President Yeltsin because its leader, Dzhokar Dudayev, wanted to break away from Russia. Finally, in December, the might of the Russian army was unleashed on the Chechen capital, Grozny. First came bombing runs by Russian jets, then the Russian army went in – 40,000 troops practically besieged the city. ITN reporters Andrew Simmons and Julian Manyon covered this dangerous story and Julian managed to obtain an exclusive interview with President Dudayev, in which he rejected Yeltsin's plans for peace talks. When Andrew and Julian reached the centre of Grozny, what they found was a moonscape of destruction, as Russian bombs and shells had flattened almost the entire city. Half a million people were made homeless. Many had left the city but others were still there – trying to survive the winter with few supplies and little proper shelter.

Above: Bill Neely reports that National guard soldiers are patrolling the streets to protect against looting. Along the coast, valuable beachouse properties have been damaged by landslides associated with the earthquake.

Above: The force of the earthquake has split slabs of concrete – and even entire houses – apart.

Woodstock '94 begins, on the 25th anniversary of the original Woodstock

Francisco Martin Duran fires 29 rounds at the White House

National Lottery launched

Russia invades Chechnya

12 August

29 October

19 November

11 December

When news of the collapse of Barings Bank emerged in February, ITN was quick to realise the scale of the story. The demise of the long-established name of Barings was interesting enough in itself, but here was a great human drama about a rogue trader, Nick Leeson, getting in above his neck and gambling on the movements of the Japanese stock market. When it went terribly wrong he got out and went on the run. It was also a story that affected everyone in Britain with a pension – his actions brought down the value of shares on the London Stock Market, reducing the value of pensions across the board.

Barings had been in existence for well over 200 years when it gave Leeson a job. Even though he had no formal qualifications he had worked at other banks, eventually being promoted to the trading floor. In the end, he lost Barings around £800 million – more than the bank's entire capital and reserves – hiding his extraordinary losses in a secret account. ITN's Asia correspondent Caroline Kerr covered the twists and turns of the story after

Below left and right: The 50th anniversary of VE-day (Victory in Europe) was celebrated in London by a huge crowd outside Buckingham Palace. After observing a two-minute silence, the Queen set off ticker tape to ignite a large beacon and turned on a laser and firework display.

An earthquake in Japan kills over 5,000 people

Barings Bank brought down by rogue trader Nick Leeson after he loses $1.4 billion

Comedian Peter Cook dies

9 January

17 January

24 February

the collapse of the bank and the subsequent hunt for Leeson. He and his wife Lisa had vanished from their luxury flat in Singapore, but finally he was tracked down and was arrested getting off a plane in Germany. Extradited to Singapore, he stood trial and was sentenced to six and a half years in jail. ITN reported on Lisa becoming an air stewardess to get cheap travel so she could go and see him. But the marriage didn't survive and nor did Barings – it was bought out by the Dutch bank ING.

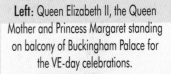

Left: Queen Elizabeth II, the Queen Mother and Princess Margaret standing on balcony of Buckingham Palace for the VE-day celebrations.

Above: Widespread devastation and fires followed the Kobe earthquake in Japan.

It was a year of big stories in the Far East. The Japanese city of Kobe was hit by a terrible earthquake. More than 5,000 people were killed and ITN's reports reflected the terrible human suffering. Most Japanese had believed their homes could withstand an earthquake. It was the costliest natural disaster in history, inflicting damage estimated at £60 billion because of the high rise, closely packed streets.

Commemorations were held to mark 50 years since the end of the Second World War in Europe. ITN staged a series of special programmes in May to mark the VE-day anniversary. There was a service at St Paul's, a dinner of European leaders at Guildhall, and appearances by the Queen on the Buckingham Palace balcony. She and other members of the royal family also joined veterans and thousands of members of the public in Hyde Park, where displays and exhibitions of wartime life were staged. ITN reporters were also in other European capitals, for their commemorations.

Above: VJ-Day marked the end of the War with Japan. On the 50th anniversary crowds gathered outside the gates of Buckingham Palace, a Lancaster bomber flew overhead, trailing red poppies over the Mall, and the day was also marked by a parade of veterans of the Second World War.

Oklahoma bombing, 168 people are killed

VE-Day 50th anniversary

Actor Hugh Grant is arrested with a prostitute by LA Police

An unprecedented heatwave hits Midwestern America, lasting for days and killing thousands

19 April

8 May

28 June

July

Above: Eton welcomes Prince William, who is to continue his education as a boarder in Manor House.

Above: Prince William gives photographers a big smile as he walks past wearing his Eton uniform.

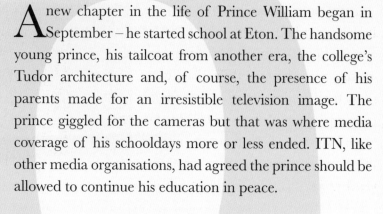

A new chapter in the life of Prince William began in September – he started school at Eton. The handsome young prince, his tailcoat from another era, the college's Tudor architecture and, of course, the presence of his parents made for an irresistible television image. The prince giggled for the cameras but that was where media coverage of his schooldays more or less ended. ITN, like other media organisations, had agreed the prince should be allowed to continue his education in peace.

However, the media's interest in his parents' private life continued. When the Queen called on Charles and Diana to 'seek an early divorce' in December, the fate of their marriage was sealed. The formal divorce itself was agreed the following year – Diana was to receive a £17 million settlement but would lose the right to be addressed as Her Royal Highness.

The trial of OJ Simpson began in January and was watched on television around the world. His arrest the previous year had been a media event too, after the bodies of his wife and a male friend of hers were discovered at her house in Brentwood in Los Angeles. Around 1,000 reporters waited to see Simpson taken into police custody but he didn't show up. Instead, television viewers were treated to the incredible spectacle of live coverage, from American news helicopters, of the police pursuit of Simpson's white Ford Bronco car along Interstate 405. It is estimated that, in the United States alone, some 95 million people watched some part of that chase. Simpson eventually drove to the house in Brentwood and surrendered.

VJ-Day 50th anniversary

Prince William starts at Eton

OJ Simpson is acquitted of the murder of his wife

Release of *Goldeneye*, starring Pierce Brosnan, the first Bond film after a six-year gap

15 August

6 September

3 October

November

The trial was covered for ITN by Bill Neely. For British television viewers, who weren't used to cameras in court, it made compulsive nightly viewing, even though OJ Simpson – America's most famous sportsman – was far less well known across the Atlantic. The end of the trial, when it came, was dramatic and controversial. It had lasted eight months – yet the jury took less than four hours to decide he was not guilty.

In Los Angeles, British actor Hugh Grant also found himself in front of the wrong kind of cameras, as he posed for a mug-shot for the LAPD. He was caught on Sunset Boulevard with a prostitute in his car and was fined US$1,200 and given two years' probation. His subsequent appearance on Jay Leno's *Tonight Show*, in which he made an unqualified apology for his 'goatish' behaviour, produced record ratings.

Above left and right: In December 1995, UN peacekeepers were chained up as 'human shields' at key points on roads and bridges, to prevent NATO air strikes against Bosnian Serb targets. They were forced to make anti-NATO statements to assembled reporters.

In Oklahoma City, at 9.02am on April 19th, a massive explosion tore apart the Alfred P. Murrah Federal Building. 168 people were killed, including 19 children. Within an hour of the explosion, Timothy McVeigh, a veteran of the Gulf war, was pulled over by an Oklahoma Highway Patrolman for not having a licence plate on his car and subsequently arrested for the bombing. Initial news reports had suggested that the attack might be the work of Middle-Eastern terrorists but it transpired that McVeigh, with at least two accomplices, had planned it to avenge the deaths of members of the Branch Davidian sect at Waco, Texas in 1993. Unrepentant, McVeigh was sentenced to death and executed by lethal injection on 11 June, 2001.

Above: The flag-draped coffin, carried by military pallbearers, at the funeral of assassinated Israeli Prime Minister Yitzhak Rabin.

Funeral of assassinated Israeli Prime Mnister Yitzhak Rabin

Toy Story is released, the first feature-length animated film that is completely computer-generated

First Beatles' reunion song, 'Free as a Bird', is released

6 November

21 November

4 December

183

The IRA's 17 month ceasefire was blown apart in February by an enormous bomb in London's docklands. Some ITN staff in the newsroom thought they heard the muffled boom, several miles away. It went off at 7pm, killing two people and causing an immense amount of damage. Warnings had been phoned through and the police were evacuating the area around the South Quay Docklands light railway station, when the bomb went off. The explosion shook the 800-foot Canary Wharf Tower, which was later evacuated.

Right: The aftermath of the Docklands bomb – a van packed with explosives had been planted in the area by the IRA and there was massive damage to buildings in the vicinity. One local resident, far right, shows reporters the glass all over his front garden. Several people were injured, and there were two deaths.

Right: Views of Manchester city centre, which was totally destroyed by an IRA bomb in June 1996. Debris covers the roads and most of the central shopping area was badly damaged. Again the explosives were packed in a van, which was left near a crowded shopping area – a tourist captured the moment of the explosion in an amateur video.

The attacks didn't stop there. The IRA exploded a similar bomb in Manchester in June; it went off outside the city's Arndale shopping centre shortly after 11am. Once again warnings were given. Once again there was massive damage to buildings. It seemed further proof that the IRA

Hilary Clinton testifies in the Whitewater scandal

IRA bomb in Canary Wharf, killed two people

Release of *Trainspotting*, starring Ewan McGregor

The second Beatles' reunion song, 'Real Love', is released

26 January

9 February

26 February

4 March

Above: During the Chechen conflict, Russian combat troops on the ground run to take up position. ITN reporter Andrew Simmons and a camera crew were on the spot to send back reports.

Above: Russian troops, with tanks, on the edge of a village – a suspected hideout for Chechen rebels. Soldiers were angry at the media presence and tried to get newsmen to leave.

was concentrating on inflicting economic damage rather than fatalities, but more than 220 people were injured.

In the breakaway Soviet Republic of Chechnya, ITN's Andrew Simmons continued to send dispatches from the capital city, Grozny, which was now firmly under Russian military control. What he and, via his filmed reports, ITN's viewers witnessed was a descent into utter chaos during which his own life was at risk more than once. Hostages were being taken daily, prisoners tortured and civilians shot at random. Over 30,000 Chechens died in the conflict, the vast majority of them civilians, plus 1,500 Russian troops. President Dudayev, the leader of the Chechen rebels, was killed by a shell fragment in April. In May, Boris Yeltsin met with representatives of the Chechen rebels for the first time and agreed to begin withdrawing Russian troops.

Above: Flares in the night sky over the village under seige. The Chechen rebels had taken some villagers as hostages.

Above: Distressed villagers, relatives of the hostages, wait for news.

Thomas Hamilton murders 16 children and a teacher in Dunblane primary school

Government announces that BSE can be transmitted to humans

Christopher Robin Milne, son of AA Milne and inspiration for Christopher Robin in *Winnie the Pooh*, dies

13 March

20 March

20 April

1996 Dunblane

Above left: Parents gather waiting for news outside Dunblane Primary School, where Thomas Hamilton slaughtered 16 children and a teacher. He walked into the school with several guns and shot at random, before turning one of the guns on himself.

Above right: Anxious parents run towards the school as news of the attack spreads around the town.

One of the most harrowing events in British history was the massacre at Dunblane. Here, in a small Scottish town, a 43-year-old local man called Thomas Hamilton entered the school's gymnasium, where a class of five- and six-year-old children were just beginning a PE lesson. Hamilton was carrying four handguns and 700 rounds of ammunition. He opened fire at random, killing 16 children and their teacher before putting the barrel of the gun into his mouth and pulling the trigger. An enquiry set up under Lord Cullen could discover no specific motive for the terrible crime, but Hamilton had previously drawn attention to himself through his unhealthy fascination with young boys. He had been reported to the police and had been barred from the Scout Association.

Colin Baker was sent to cover the incident for ITN. He found it one of the most harrowing assignments of his career, which had included reporting on some of the world's darkest tragedies. Colin's award-winning coverage from Dunblane was exemplary in its sensitivity towards a community that was traumatised by grief.

Russian President Boris Yeltsin meets Chechen rebels to negotiate a cease-fire

An IRA bomb devastates Manchester City Centre

Dolly the sheep, cloned from an adult cell, is born

27 May

15 June

5 July

Reporters often look back at how their work appeared on air but Colin said he never wanted to see again the pictures of parents running to find out if their children were among those who had died.

Fiona Armstrong

Fiona Armstrong's first job in broadcasting was in 1980, when she worked as a reporter for *Radio 210* in Reading. Before that she had been editor of the London University student newspaper, after studying German there. She joined the BBC in 1982, working in Manchester on *North West Tonight*. In 1985 she moved to Border Television to present another regional news programme, *Lookaround*. She went to ITN in 1987 to work on *News at One*, *News at Ten* and primarily *News at 5.45*. She covered the visit of the Prince and Princess of Wales to West Africa and also reported on the suffering of children with AIDS in Uganda. She was involved in a serious road accident in 1990, and despite neck injuries, managed to comfort frightened children in another vehicle until help arrived. In 1992 she moved to GMTV as their main female presenter. In 1994 she returned to Border TV to present a series of programmes about her favourite hobby called *Fiona on Fishing*. She has written a book on fly fishing and also published *The Commuter's Cookbook*. Fiona is now a news presenter with *ITV Border* in Carlisle.

Above: Scientists worried by the effect of global warming in Antarctica have been studying the Larsen ice shelf and a large ice cliff. Rifts in the ice and large sections falling into the sea indicate that the ridge is breaking apart.

Bill Clinton wins a second term as President

The Summer Olympics open in Atlanta, Georgia

The Prince and Princess of Wales are formally divorced

The Taliban capture Kabul, capital of Afghanistan

19 July

28 August

27 September

5 November

Above: The tunnel in Paris where Princess Diana was fatally injured in a car accident. The column still bears the marks of the impact of the limousine.

Far right: Diana, Princess of Wales, Queen of Hearts.

The biggest news story of the year broke late at night on Saturday August 31st. First reports were of a car crash in Paris involving Princess Diana and her friend Dodi Fayed. Dodi was reported dead soon after news of the crash came, but some early accounts from the scene said the Princess had walked away. As ITN staff hurried into the building no one was sure what lay ahead.

The Princess had been staying in Paris with Dodi, the son of the owner of London's famous Harrods department store, Mohamed Al Fayed. They had had dinner at Paris's Ritz Hotel. On leaving, Dodi, angered at the presence of 'paparazzi' photo-graphers outside the hotel, de-cided to change the car, driver and route. They set off in a Mercedes Benz, driven by Henri Paul, a Ritz Security Officer, and accompanied by the Princess's bodyguard, Trevor Rees-Jones. Despite these efforts, they were still pursued by photographers and the car entered a tunnel beside the Seine, at the Pont d'Alma, at high speed. For reasons that may never be known, the car went out of control and collided with the 13th concrete pillar in the centre of the tunnel. Neither the Princess nor Dodi Fayed, who were seated in the back of the car, were wearing seat belts. Despite desperate efforts by French emergency services, both of them died as a result of their injuries, as did the driver. Mr Rees-Jones was the sole survivor.

Left: The funeral cortège after the service, the hearse covered in flowers thrown by the thousands of people lining the route of its journey to her final resting place at Althorp.

Increased activity of the volcano on Montserrat leads many residents to be evacuated

Reformed Fleetwood Mac release their album, *The Dance*, a recording of a live performance

Princess Diana is killed in a car crash in Paris

August

19 August

31 August

The public outpouring of grief was unparalleled. Within hours, crowds had gathered outside Kensington Palace, Princess Diana's London home, and a vast sea of flowers soon covered the garden. Nicholas Owen, reporting for ITN, was struck by the number of people, but also by how silent they were. It was almost as if they were in a state of shock.

Left: Prince Philip, Prince William, Earl Spencer, Prince Harry and Prince Charles follow the coffin on foot as it moves towards Westminster Abbey.

Later, *Channel 4 News* was to reveal the feud within the royal family over the arrangement's for Diana's funeral. The Queen was said to want a private funeral. It was Prince Charles who wanted it to be a state occasion. *Channel 4 News* discovered the Prince had enlisted Tony Blair's help to get his way.

Below: The coffin, covered in the Welsh flag, is borne on a gun carriage to the service. London came to a standstill as thousands gathered along the route to pay their respects.

By now ITN was producing television news for three different and competing broadcasters. *Five News* was launched in March, presented by Kirsty Young, perching on the edge of a desk and free to move around the studio. *Five News* promised a more pacy, accessible form of reporting. More emphasis was given to entertainment news but ITN rejected any suggestion of trivialising the news agenda.

Aided by disaffection with the Conservative government – who were dogged by allegations of corruption and long-running divisions over Europe, New Labour achieved a landslide victory over John Major in the May general election. At 43, Blair became Britain's youngest Prime Minister since Lord Liverpool in 1812.

Major forest fires across Indonesia

Mother Teresa dies in Calcutta

Funeral of Princess Diana at Westminster Abbey

Release of *Titantic*, starring Leonardo DiCaprio and Kate Winslet

September

5 September

6 September

19 December

Above: US president Bill Clinton testifies under oath in the Monica Lewinsky affair.

Trevor McDonald and some of the *News at Ten* production team flew off to Washington at the start of the year, to present the programme from there as President Bill Clinton fought attempts to force him out of office. Reports of his affair with White House intern Monica Lewinsky had surfaced first on the internet and then in American newspapers and, at one point, it looked like he might resign. ITN wanted to present *News at Ten* from Washington if he did. Even if he didn't, the story of sex, lies by the President and secret tapes of Ms Lewinsky talking about their relationship was compelling.

The *News at Ten* team headed from the airport into ITN's Washington bureau, where they would be working over the next days. They had only been there a couple of hours when news agency reports appeared from London saying the Queen Mother had fallen and was badly hurt. For a woman of her age – she was 97 at the time – it was a serious accident. Here was a dilemma for ITN. Should Trevor stay in Washington or should he return to London in case the worst happened? Trevor flew back to London by Concorde early the following morning. By the time of that night's *News at Ten*, it was clear the Queen Mother's life wasn't in danger but she did need a hip replacement. President Clinton survived too – he faced impeachment hearings later in the year but he was not forced out of office. The Queen Mother was in hospital for just 23 days and ITN was there to film her leaving as she walked down the stairs, helped only by a stick and wearing high-heeled shoes.

Above: Singer George Michael smiles and jokes briefly with reporters as he arrives at London airport.

Back in the US, singer George Michael was arrested for 'engaging in a lewd act' in a public lavatory in Beverley Hills, California. He was fined US$800 and given 80 hours community service. In 2004 he released 'Patience', which went to Number One in the UK.

The *Lunar Prospector* spacecraft is launched into orbit round the moon, and later finds evidence of frozen water on the surface

US President Bill Clinton's affair with White House intern Monica Lewinsky is revealed in the press

On US television Bill Clinton denies he had sex with 'that woman'

Hurricanes hit Florida causing massive damage and 42 deaths

6 January

21 January

26 January

23 February

Mark Austin

Mark Austin is the main presenter of the ITV *News at 10.30*, taking over from Sir Trevor McDonald this year. Mark is also co-presenter of the *ITV Evening News*, with Mary Nightingale – a job he has been doing since 2002. Mark's first job was as a general reporter for the Bournemouth *Evening Echo* between 1976 and 1980. He then joined the BBC television newsroom as a script writer, before becoming a reporter in 1982. He moved to sports reporting three years later. In 1986 he joined ITN, initially as a sports reporter, but he reported from the Gulf during Iraq's invasion of Kuwait in 1990, and from Bahrain during operation 'Desert Storm' the following year. In the mid 1990s, he was reporting from Africa, covering Nelson Mandela's election victory and the terrible civil war in Rwanda. He also worked as *ITV News*' Asia correspondent, reporting from Hong Kong on the handover to China in 1997. He received an International Emmy Award for his coverage of the catastrophic floods in Mozambique in 2000 and, in 2001, he covered the 9/11 attacks on New York City.

Above: The Queen Mother smiles and waves for the cameras as she leaves hospital after her hip replacement operation. She had been out of action for only just over three weeks.

George Michael is arrested in a public toilet in California for 'lewd conduct'

Apple unveils the iMac

Frank Sinatra dies

Geri Halliwell announces her departure from the Spice Girls

7 April

7 May

14 May

30 May

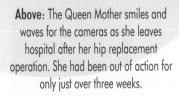

Above left and right: ITN's News at Ten had been broadcast for 32 years, but it finally came to an end in March 1999. During those years, newscasters such as Andrew Gardner, Reginald Bosanquet and Alastair Burnet had brought the day's news into living rooms across the country. The Independent Television Commission (ITC) had decided that 'direct intervention by regulator to dictate the precise scheduling of a programme even an institution such as News at Ten looks increasingly inappropriate'.

News at Ten's three-month trial finally came to an end after 32 years. During that time it had been Britain's most popular news programme, but ITV believed its schedule needed to alter to compete for viewers. Trevor McDonald and his production team moved to an earlier slot for the *ITV Evening News* at 6.30pm and a new programme was created at 11pm, the *ITV Nightly News*, presented by Dermot Murnaghan.

With most of Britain shrouded by cloud, the best pictures of the first total eclipse in Britain for 72 years came from an RAF Hercules flying above the cloud cover. Cameraman Eugene Campbell was on board the plane and the flight was timed with military precision so the Hercules would be in the right place at the right time. The entire sequence of the moon passing in front of

Joe DiMaggio, former baseball player and husband of Marilyn Monroe, dies

Clinton is acquitted in his impeachment trial

Hereditary peerages abolished by Labour

Two Libyans suspected of the 1988 PanAm bomb over Lockerbie are handed over to Scottish authorities

12 February

8 March

16 March

5 April

the sun and away again was filmed 'hand held', without a tripod or camera mount. The pictures were used on ITN's live programmes on ITV, Channel Four, and Channel Five, and were beamed around the world. The eclipse was meant to be at its most complete in the West Country but there were clouds there too, obscuring the view of many people. Thousands of pairs of special sunglasses had been produced to make sure people didn't stare straight into the sunlight.

The former Conservative cabinet minister Jonathan Aitken who, it was once said, could end up in Downing Street, found himself in jail instead. He was sentenced to 18 months for perjury and conspiracy to pervert the course of justice. ITN's court artist Priscilla Coleman produced the sketches of Aitken in the dock – which symbolised his fall from grace. He had resigned from John Major's Government after allegations that he had violated Parliamentary rules of conduct by allowing a Saudi businessman to pay for him to stay at the Ritz Hotel in Paris. He said he would use 'the simple sword of truth and the trusty shield of British fair play' to sue his accusers and he began a libel action against the *Guardian* newspaper and Granada Television. He claimed his wife had been with him and it was she who had paid the bill, but the action collapsed when the bill from the Ritz was produced, passed to the *Guardian* by the hotel's owner, Mohamed Al Fayed. It transpired that Mrs Aitken had not been in Paris but in Switzerland, dropping off their daughter at school. It also transpired that Mr Aitken had been prepared to have his teenage daughter lie under oath to support his alibi. He was declared bankrupt and his trustees were constrained to settle various actions against the magazine *Private Eye* which had accused him, accurately, of being a serial liar.

Above: These two are taking no chances. Even during an eclipse, looking directly at the sun could damage or destroy eyesight.

Above far left: The moment of totality – a view of the sun at the moment of eclipse, as seen across parts of southern Britain in August 1999.

Above: Artist's impression of Jonathan Aitken in the witness box during his trial for perjury. He was later sentenced to 18 months in jail.

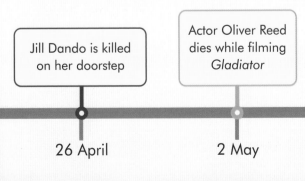

Jill Dando is killed on her doorstep

Actor Oliver Reed dies while filming *Gladiator*

Release of *Notting Hill*, starring Julia Roberts and Hugh Grant

Manchester United complete their unprecedented treble by winning UEFA – they had already won the Premier and the FA Cup

26 April

2 May

13 May

26 May

Above: George Harrison in London – the former member of The Beatles was attacked with a knife in his own home, but managed to fight the intruder off.

Above: Prince William stirs up some controversy by going out with the Beaufort Hunt.

A series of bizarre attacks made the news in 1999. BBC News Presenter Jill Dando was shot dead on the doorstep of her home in Fulham, in South West London, on the morning of April 26th. Her killer was later identified as Barry George, an unemployed man with a severe personality disorder. It was claimed that he had previously stalked the Princess of Wales.

Former Beatle George Harrison and his wife, Olivia, were viciously attacked by an intruder at their mansion in Henley-on-Thames in Oxfordshire. Both survived, and their assailant, 34-year-old Michael Abram, was tried for attempted murder. Psychiatrists called to give evidence said that Abram believed that he was possessed by Harrison and

Jonathan Aitken is jailed for 18 months for perjury

8 June

John F Kennedy Jnr is killed in a plane crash

16 July

Solar eclipse across much of Europe, the Middle East and southern Asia

11 August

Ladbroke Grove rail crash – 31 die

5 October

was convinced he was a witch. Abram was found not guilty by reason of insanity and committed to a secure hospital.

Prince William took the controversial decision to join his father for a day with the Beaufort Hunt. A ban on hunting was already in the offing and some saw it as a statement intended to show his opposition to the plan.

His uncle, Prince Edward, meanwhile got married to PR consultant Sophie Rhys-Jones and the couple gave an eve of wedding interview to Trevor McDonald. Prince Edward summed up the key to their happiness 'We manage to have a good laugh about things most of the time,' he said, 'and we happen to love each other which is the most important thing of all'.

Above: With Issue 3007, *Dandy* becomes the world's longest running comic.

Above: As a heatwave hits Russia, people take to the beaches in swimwear, enjoying the unexpected sunshine.

Above: The weather has a more serious effect on Russian forests, some of which catch fire. Fire-fighters battle to contain the blaze.

Westlife release their debut album, *Westlife*

Australians vote to keep the Queen as their Head of State

Former Beatle George Harrison is stabbed in his home

Millennium Dome opened

1 November

6 November

29 December

31 December

2000s

NEW MILLENNIUM

The new Millennium brought new opportunities for ITN. The company launched its own *ITN News Channel* to bring viewers 24-hour coverage with its established team of reporters. Alongside that, ITN news became available on the new generation of 3G mobile phones. As ITN approached its 50th anniversary, it continued to provide world-beating coverage of the new century's darkest days.

ITN 50
The first 50 years

Above: Despite the hype, the millennium bug did not cause the promised havoc in shops and offices.

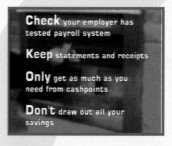

Check your employer has tested payroll system

Keep statements and receipts

Only get as much as you need from cashpoints

Don't draw out all your savings

Above: ITN does its bit to try to stem the tide of fear and panic, with a few sensible words of advice.

Diary items – those news stories such as court cases, parliamentary debates and summits, which have a predictable starting date – are not much easier to spot than the start of the new Millennium. So ITN had plenty of time to plan its coverage. Trevor McDonald celebrated New Year's Eve and the start of New Year's Day in the studio, as 1999 became 2000 around the world and ITN had reporters across time zones to cover the celebrations.

In the run up to the big day, ITN had covered warnings from IT experts that the Millennium bug would bring cash machines, lifts, traffic lights and, of course, office and home computers to a halt if their software wasn't modified to cope with the change in date. In the end, those warnings about the Y2K bug proved to be wrong.

The new Millennium brought a new ITN service – its own 24-hour TV news station called the **ITN News Channel**. It had its own team of producers and reporters, but its strength lay in the reporting power of established ITN correspondents. The channel ran many of their reports, but also took live updates from them at the scene of breaking stories. Setting up the new service hadn't been without its problems – unions had been worried that journalists and camera crews would end up having to be available 24 hours a day to subsidise ITN's expansion. There was talk of industrial action but the company gave sufficient assurances to head it off.

In Northern Ireland, massive protests at Drumcree made for some dramatic images when members of the Protestant Orange Order were prevented from marching away from an annual church service along their 'traditional' route which led through a Roman Catholic area. *ITV News'* Ireland correspondent, John Irvine, covered the confrontations. They were

Dr Harold Shipman is found guilty of murdering at least 15 of 365 suspected victims

31 January

London Eye opens

8 March

Britney Spears releases her single 'Oops! I Did It Again'

April

Millennium Bridge opens

May

ugly and violent, despite the intervention of US President Bill Clinton, who valiantly attempted to move the process of establishing peace in the province forward. Troops were brought back onto the streets of Belfast for the first time in two years.

John Irvine

John Irvine was born and educated in Belfast. His first job was with the local paper in Omagh. After four years there, he became a reporter for Ulster Television until he joined ITN in 1994. He was *ITV News'* correspondent for Ireland for five years and covered many stories of sectarian violence, including Drumcree and the Shankhill Road bombing. He became Middle East correspondent in 2002 and reported from Baghdad, covering Saddam Hussein's election victory that year. He has also reported from Jerusalem, covering some of the worst atrocities in the continuing conflict between Israeli forces and Palestinians. He managed to report directly from Ramallah, the headquarters of the PLO leader Yasser Arafat, during the Israeli occupation there. During the second Gulf War he reported from Baghdad, giving nightly eye-witness accounts of the bombing of the city. He was the first journalist to greet American troops when they reached Baghdad and received a Royal Television Society award as Journalist of the Year for his coverage. He become Asia correspondent for *ITV News* in 2003.

Above: Floods across Southern England in November 2000 caused thousands of pounds worth of damage, while many had to be evacuated as the water rose.

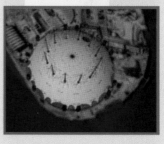

Above: Views of the Millennium Dome, which welcomed thousands of visitors throughout the first year of the new millennium – or the last year of the old, depending on your point of view.

Gladiator, starring Russell Crowe and Oliver Reed, is released

Tate Modern opens

Birth of Leo Blair, son of Prime Minister Tony Blair and Cherie Booth

Robert Runcie, the Archbishop of Canterbury, dies

5 May

12 May

20 May

11 July

Above left, middle and right: The Queen Mother and Prince Charles wave to cheering crowds as they head towards Buckingham Palace on the occasion of the Queen Mother's 100th birthday. She looked very elegant in a pale blue outfit.

Above: Author JK Rowling hit the jackpot with her stories of a trainee wizard called Harry Potter.

To the delight of her many admirers, the Queen Mother celebrated her 100th birthday – and ITN stole a march on the BBC in its coverage of the commemorative pageant in Horse Guards Parade at the end of July. The Queen Mother wanted the event to be a look back at how life had changed in the century since she was born, through a series of floats. The BBC said it did not want to broadcast the pageant live but preferred to mark her birthday on August 4th as usual – one reason, reported in the newspapers, was said to be that the event would clash with the Australian soap opera, *Neighbours*. There was an outcry among royalists but the BBC refused to change its mind, so, with the support of Prince Charles, Buckingham Palace turned to ITN. Trevor McDonald presented the special programme, with John Suchet providing the commentary during the two-hour event.

George W. Bush became the 43rd President of the United States – just. On the night of the count, even American TV stations said his Democratic rival, Senator Al Gore, had won. Due to the nature of the American electoral system, the election ended up being decided in Florida, where some 10,000

An Air France Concorde crashes soon after take-off from Charles de Gaulle Airport killing all 109 aboard and 5 on the ground

100th birthday of Queen Elizabeth, the Queen Mother

The Russian submarine *Kursk* sinks, all 118 crew die

Protests about the cost of fuel, across the UK

25 July

4 August

12 August

September

votes out of six million separated Mr Bush from Mr Gore, on the first count. On a recount, Mr Bush won by 537 votes. The Democrats wanted a manual recount but the Supreme Court upheld Mr Bush's victory.

On October 18th, a Kings Cross to Leeds train came off the tracks at 115 miles per hour, at Hatfield in Hertfordshire, the crash killing four passengers and injuring a further 70 people. By the following day, an investigation by *Channel 4 News* had managed to establish a broken rail was to blame.

The year's sporting headlines were dominated largely by Americans – Lance Armstrong, Tiger Woods and Venus Williams – but the arts belonged to the British with the opening of the new Tate Modern gallery and the publication of the first Harry Potter novel. The adventures of the young wizard were to make author JK Rowling richer than the Queen.

Above left, middle and right: A crowd of thousands in the Mall, to see a balcony appearance by members of the Royal family. Amidst all the pomp and ceremony, ordinary people expressed their birthday greetings.

Above: The crowds of people walking over the new Millennium Bridge caused it to sway too much, and several walkers suffered motion sickness. The bridge was quickly closed for repairs.

Summer Olympics open in Sydney

Hatfield rail crash

Widespread flooding across England and Wales

George W. Bush is finally confirmed as the new President of the US after several recounts

15 September

17 October

3 November

12 December

The first anyone at ITN knew of the attacks of 11 September was a news agency report flashing on computer screens saying a light aircraft had crashed into the World Trade Center in New York. Within what seemed like seconds, American television stations turned live cameras on the building and journalists in the newsroom could see the smoke coming out of the North Tower. It seemed like a bizarre accident. But when the second plane hit the South Tower, as everyone watched, it was terrifyingly clear it was no accident. Within a few minutes ITV agreed to ITN broadcasting a newsflash. Kirsty Young, by now a presenter on the *ITV Evening News*, rushed down to the studio. She was due to be on air for 45 seconds. *ITV News* stayed on air for the next five hours as the terrible events unfolded. A third aircraft, American Airlines Flight 77, was flown into the Pentagon, America's defence headquarters, in Washington DC and a fourth plane, United Airlines Flight 93, crashed in a field near to Shanksville in Somerset County, Pennsylvania, after passengers tried to storm the cockpit. President Bush was visiting a school in Sarasota, Florida, when word was brought to him of the attacks. There was speculation that an attack might be planned for the White House – which may have been the intended target of the fourth aircraft – so the President was flown to

Above: The New York skyline dominated by the Twin Towers of the New York World Trade Center.

Right: The skyline after the terrible events of 9/11, in which thousands of people died.

George W Bush succeeds Bill Clinton as President of the US

An earthquake in India destroys most of the historical city of Gujarat and kills 20,000

Start of an outbreak of foot and mouth disease in Britain

Singer Harry Secombe dies

20 January

26 January

20 February

11 April

Barksdale Airforce Base in Louisiana and then to US Strategic Command at Offutt, Nebraska, in the Presidential jet *Airforce One*. From there he finally returned to Washington in his *Marine One* helicopter.

In any breaking news story, accurate pictures, information and eye witness accounts are hard to come by but, soon after going on air, Kirsty mentioned to producers that her husband, Nick, was in New York. He was contacted and ended up talking to her live on the phone, but she only referred to him as Nick Jones. Nick described in calm but dramatic detail what he could see. It was only after their lengthy conversation ended that Kirsty told viewers. 'That was Nick Jones. He's in New York on business, and the reason I know that is because he's my husband'.

ITV News remained on air as the Twin Towers came crashing down. Production staff in the control room could scarcely believe what they were seeing on the TV monitors in front of them.

Plans were already being made to send more reporters to New York to help Washington correspondent James Mates cover the story. But of course no flights were allowed into New York for several days. James went on to produce some of the most powerful reports ever seen on ITN, using pictures of the explosions and office workers jumping from windows to escape the extraordinary heat inside. By November, Jon Snow and his *Channel 4 News* crew became the first television journalists to be allowed access to the site of Ground Zero.

Above: The memorial service at Ground Zero a year on. Former New York Mayor Rudolph Giuliani began to read a list of those who died, and at 08.46 a bell was rung to mark the moment when the first plane crashed into the North Tower. At the end of the ceremony, the 'Last Post' was played.

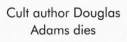

Cult author Douglas Adams dies

The Real IRA bomb Ealing centre, causing widespread damage

Two hijacked airliners are flown into the Twin Towers in New York, almost 2,800 are killed

11 May

2 August

11 September

Right: Relatives show pictures of their loved ones, all lost in the terrorist attack on the Twin Towers.

The number of those killed on 9/11 was almost 2,800 – in the Twin Towers of the World Trade Center, at the Pentagon and on board the four planes. At first it seemed the number might be higher. ITN reporters followed the terrible anguish of families trying to find out if their loved ones had lived or died. Relatives posted photographs on lamp posts and street corners in a desperate attempt to get information. It transpired, from mobile phone communications, that the hijackers had used various noxious sprays and knives to threaten and overpower passengers and aircrew. No one on any of the aircraft survived but it is thought that there were, in total, 19 hijackers involved. They belonged, or at least subscribed to, the beliefs and aims of the Al Qaeda movement, the symbolic leader of which was, and remains, Osama Bin Laden. It wasn't just an attack on America but on the western world and its suffering was shared worldwide. In the UK, relatives and friends grieved for the 67 British victims of the attacks.

Above: Freed British plane-spotter Lesley Coppin embracing relatives after arriving back in Britain. A group of plane-spotters had been accused of spying and imprisoned in Greece, after taking pictures near a military air base.

American attack on Afghanistan begins

Apple releases the iPod

Release of the animated film *Monsters, Inc*

7 October

23 October

2 November

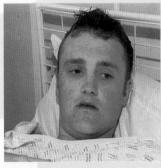

Above: Richard Seaman lying in hospital after the Ealing bomb attack by the Real IRA.

Left: Wrecked shops and mangled wreckage in the roads of Ealing in the aftermath of the bomb.

Left: ITN's famous symbol gets a facelift, when abseilers are brought in to clean Big Ben's clock face.

Paul McCartney releases his album *Driving Rain*

Release of the first Harry Potter film, *Harry Potter and the Philosopher's Stone*, starring Daniel Radcliffe and Emma Watson

Former Beatle George Harrison dies

Enron files for bankruptcy

12 November

16 November

29 November

2 December

Above: A shopkeeper in Paris inspects an example of the new Euro currency, after it is launched in twelve European countries at the beginning of 2002.

Above: George W Bush poses with Prime Minister Tony Blair MP outside Chequers, during his official visit to the UK.

As clocks struck midnight to usher in the New Year, small knots of people gathered around automatic cash dispensers across continental Europe to witness the miracle of the Euro. Cash machines, which had lain dormant for the preceding 24 hours, suddenly came to life and delivered new bank notes that could be used in 12 countries, from the Mediterranean to the Baltic. *ITV News'* Europe correspondent, Bill Neely, was in Paris to film the big switch. Economics editor Caroline Kerr explained what it meant for people in Britain and showed that Euros would be welcome in some places in Britain – including the London toy shop, Hamleys.

In October, *Channel 4 News* revealed that there had been four warnings to police that the Real IRA were planning to bomb Omagh in 1998. A police ombudsman's report had already revealed two tip-offs, given 11 days and 3 days before. However, an investigation by Alex Thomson revealed a further two – one four days before the bombing and the other the day before.

Explosions tore through the tourist resort of Kuta in Bali, killing over 200 people, most of them tourists and most of them young. Al Qaeda was thought, initially, to be responsible but it is now believed that an Indonesian Islamic Fundamentalist group called Jemaah Islamiah was to blame. *ITV News'* Julian Manyon reported from Bali and spoke to British survivors desperately searching for missing loved ones.

Zimbabwe was suspended from the Commonwealth due to President Robert Mugabe's increasingly erratic and eccentric behaviour. Great concern had been expressed, internationally, over the conduct of the election in March, with accusations of coercion and vote-rigging. Amnesty International made numerous accusations against Mr Mugabe for

Euro launched to replace national currencies in 12 countries of Europe

1 January

Millennium Bridge reopens after excessive vibration has been fixed

February

Princess Margaret dies

9 February

Zimbabwe is suspended from the Commonwealth because of human rights abuses

March

violations of human rights and discrimination against a number of minority groups, including white farmers. Mr Mugabe was operating a policy of what he called land reform. What it amounted to was turning a blind eye to his supporters driving white farmers off their land.

Lawrence McGinty

Lawrence McGinty's first job as a science journalist was as assistant editor of *Chemistry in Britain* in 1973, having gained a degree in Zoology at Liverpool University. He moved to the *New Scientist* magazine in 1974, progressing from technology editor to news editor. He won a Queen's Silver Jubilee Award for services to science journalism in 1978. In 1982 he joined ITN as Science correspondent for *Channel 4 News* before becoming Science Editor on *ITV News* in 1987. He has reported from the Antarctic, covered the capture of an escaped Beluga whale in the Black Sea, and was the first TV journalist to speak underwater – in a specially adapted diving helmet – while reporting on the wrecks of ships from the Imperial German Fleet sunk at Scapa Flow. In 1986 he was granted a Fellowship of the Association of British Science Writers and he won a Royal Television Society Award for his coverage of the King's Cross fire in 1987. In 1992 he covered the drug scandals at the Olympics in Barcelona. He has provided specialist reports on the loss of the Space Shuttle *Challenger*, the explosion at the Chernobyl nuclear reactor and the Zeebrugge ferry disaster as well as a number of medical reports on BSE, CJD and AIDS. In 2000 he won an International Emmy for his part in reporting the floods in Mozambique.

Above and below: At their headquarters in London, members voted to suspend Zimbabwe from the Commonwealth due to President Robert Mugabe's behaviour. Amongst other charges, Mugabe, seen above with his supporters, was accused of human rights violations and persecution of minority groups.

Queen Elizabeth, the Queen Mother dies

Siege in Church of the Nativity in Bethlehem, after Israeli forces surround Palestinians holding 200 hostages

Release of *Spider-Man*, starring Tobey Maguire, Kirsten Dunst and Willem Dafoe

Former President Jimmy Carter becomes the first US President to visit Cuba since 1959

30 March

2 April

3 May

12 May

Above left and right: The funeral of Queen Elizabeth the Queen Mother in Westminster Abbey in April 2002. One of the best-loved of the Royal Family, she was mourned not only by her close relatives but by most of the nation.

Below: Queen Elizabeth II listens to the service celebrating her mother's life.

What should have been a happy year for the Queen, her Golden Jubilee, was overshadowed by personal sadness, with the death of both her younger sister and her mother. Princess Margaret had suffered a stroke the previous year, which had impaired her movement and her sight. She suffered another on February 8th and died the following day. ITN covered her death and the struggle of the Queen Mother, who had herself been unwell, to be at the Princess's funeral. The Queen Mother had been suffering from a chest infection since Christmas, but she chose to make the journey from Sandringham to Windsor by helicopter, against the advice of the Queen. She died less than two months later – an era in British public life had ended. ITN covered her funeral on *ITV News* with Trevor McDonald presenting and John Suchet providing the commentary. ITN's coverage was not one of sadness for a life lost, but one of thanksgiving for a long life of public service.

Eminem releases his album *The Eminem Show*

Queen Elizabeth II's Golden Jubilee celebrations

Investigation of the financial affairs of US domestic guru Martha Stewart begins

England lose to Brazil in the quarter finals of the World Cup, Brazil go on to win

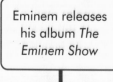

28 May

June

6 June

21 June

Prince Charles chose ITN rather than the BBC to record his television tribute to his grandmother, in what was seen as a mark of his disapproval at the BBC's coverage of her death. In his tribute the Prince talked about her sense of humour. 'Above all,' he said, 'she saw the funny side of life... Oh, how I shall miss those laughs'.

When the week of the Golden Jubilee finally arrived the mood of Britain's monarchists lifted. There were three days of celebration since there was an additional bank holiday specially for the occasion. Weeks of preparation had gone into ITN's coverage and they were rewarded with amazing scenes outside Buckingham Palace as one million cheering people crammed into the Mall. There may never be anything like it again, but for a few hours it seemed the whole of Britain was behind its monarchy.

Above: Guards in ceremonial uniform carry the coffin at the funeral of Princess Margaret, which took place in February 2002.

Inset: A host of planes, including Concorde, a Tristar flanked by Tornados, and a Nimrod escorted by two Canberras, fly past Buckingham Palace in a salute to Queen Elizabeth II during the Golden Jubilee celebrations.

Left: Thousands fill the Mall during the celebrations, waving Union Jack flags and singing 'Land of Hope and Glory' and then the National Anthem. Queen Elizabeth, Prince Philip, Prince Charles and Princes William and Harry appeared on the balcony of Buckingham Palace to wave to the crowds.

| Large areas of Europe are flooded, causing much damage and killing hundreds | Terrorist bombs in Bali kill more than 200 holidaymakers | UN weapons inspectors arrive in Iraq | The Iraq weapons declaration made to the UN Security Council is deemed incomplete |

August   12 October   18 November   7 December

Above and below: A mass of demonstrators, holding up placards, marches through central London during the anti-war with Iraq rally. This was the largest rally held to date on British soil and included anti-war religious groups from both Christian and Muslim organisations.

That Britain would join America's war on Iraq was never in doubt at the beginning of 2003. The questions was: when would it start? A million people took to the streets of London to try to persuade the Government to change its mind. In the meantime, *Channel 4 News* obtained Saddam Hussein's first Western television interview for more than a decade, conducted by the Labour MP and peace activist Tony Benn. Whatever the motives behind Mr Benn's interview, the world had been waiting to hear what the Iraqi leader would have to say on issues such as Iraq's links with Al Qaeda and the programme's ratings went up 50% that night.

The American and British military operations in Iraq lasted three weeks and cost ITN the lives of four of its staff. Never before had ITN lost anyone in a war zone, though there had been many close calls.

ITV News reporter Terry Lloyd was no stranger to Iraq. In 1988 he had revealed to the world Saddam Hussein's gassing of his own people after he discovered the bodies of Kurds in the town of Halabja in Northern Iraq. Now, as the war began, he was to travel through Iraq independently – not as one of the embedded correspondents operating within limits set by the British or American forces. He and his crew were aiming to be the first into Basra in Southern Iraq. He was travelling in one car with cameraman Daniel Demoustier, while a second cameraman, Fred Nerac, and their translator, Hussein Osman, were in a second car. They drove through checkpoints towards Basra when an Iraqi vehicle pulled up alongside them. At

US space shuttle *Columbia* explodes on re-entering Earth's atmosphere

Ozzy Osbourne releases his album *Essential Ozzy Osbourne*

Worldwide protests against the Iraq War

Adam Faith dies

1 February

11 February

15 February

8 March

that point their cars got caught in crossfire – American troops may have believed they were Iraqis and opened fire. Daniel Demoustier survived. Terry did not. His body was recovered later but Fred Nerac and Hussein Osman were missing, presumed dead. ITN also lost distinguished *Channel 4 News* Foreign Affairs correspondent Gaby Rado, who fell to his death from the roof of a hotel at Sulaymaniyah, in Northern Iraq.

Back in London, ITN was broadcasting special programmes every night at 9pm on ITV to cover the latest developments. For most of the war, Trevor McDonald presented the programme from Kuwait City. At one point he had to put his gas mask on while the programme was on air, when air raid sirens went off.

When the war finally ended, *ITV News* correspondent John Irvine obtained the coup of the conflict – he was the first journalist to see the advancing American troops arrive in Baghdad. John had woken up with what he called 'a bout of Baghdad belly', when his cameraman, Phil Bye, knocked on the door to tell him that the word was that the Americans were not far away. Although they knew the situation could be dangerous, they trusted the Iraqi people not to turn on them. They headed out from the hotel with their flak jackets on and drove until they came to a flyover and found American troops chatting to a group of Iraqis. The ITN team walked towards them with their hands on their heads and said they were journalists. An American officer beckoned them over and John shook his hand and said, 'Welcome to Baghdad'. Later that day a statue of Saddam Hussein was pulled down by jubilant Iraqis in a square right in front of the hotel that many journalists were using as their base in Baghdad, so the world was able to watch the symbolic end of the war.

Above: The demonstrators marched into Hyde Park, where a stage was set up for various speakers, including Charles Kennedy MP and model and peace campaigner Bianca Jagger.

Above: In December, a US military spokesman announced the capture of Iraqi President Saddam Hussein.

World Health Organisation issues a global alert on a new highly contagious disease, SARS

British and US forces invade Iraq

Baghdad and Basra are taken, and the US declares the Iraq War over

12 March

20 March

2nd May

Above and left: In Hong Kong, the SARS (Severe Acute Respiratory Syndrome) virus was causing panic. Many people wore masks to protect themselves, and there were fears that with today's global travel, the outbreak would quickly spread around the world.

Above: Ewan McGregor and Nicole Kidman wait to meet Prince Charles at the film premiere of *Moulin Rouge*.

International travel had only slowly recovered after the 9/11 attacks on the World Trade Center but in March came a new danger attached to long haul flying. The World Health Organisation issued a warning about a new, highly contagious and deadly disease called Severe Acute Respiratory Syndrome, or SARS, with symptoms similar to those of pneumonia. It had broken out in China but then spread across the Far East, to Hong Kong, Taiwan, and Singapore. One case was also discovered in Canada. The spread of the disease was contained, but the airline industry suffered again.

Release of *Pirates of the Caribbean*, starring Johnny Depp, Orlando Bloom and Kiera Knightley

9 July

Body of Dr David Kelly, a weapons expert on Iraq, is found, leading to the Hutton inquiry

18 July

Last commercial flight of Concorde

24 October

In Australia, the England Rugby team had their supporters back home on the edge of their sofas in the final of the World Cup. Jonny Wilkinson became a national hero when he kicked the drop goal that won England the cup in the closing moments of the game. When the triumphant squad returned, ITN cameras lined their processional route along London's Oxford Street and into Trafalgar Square. Three quarters of a million people turned out to welcome them back. Later ITN cameras caught up with the players when they attended receptions at both Downing Street and Buckingham Palace.

Left: The victorious England Rugby Union team attend receptions at Downing Street, and later at Buckingham Palace, after winning the Rugby Union World Cup.

Lady Louise Windsor, daughter of the Earl and Countess of Wessex, is born

England wins Rugby Union World Cup

Former Iraqi dictator Saddam Hussein is captured

Cold Mountain, starring Nicole Kidman and Jude Law, is released

8 November

22 November

13 December

25 December

Above: Injured passengers being tended to on the track after bombs were placed at three Madrid railway stations. Later, Al-Qaeda claimed responsibility for the attacks.

In March, a total of 10 bombs were placed on board four rush hour trains, all heading into Madrid's main station. 191 people were killed and, initially, the Spanish authorities suspected that the Basque separatist group *Eta* was responsible. It transpired, however, that Al Qaeda was once more behind the killing. Jon Snow presented *Channel 4 News* live from Madrid and the programme's report of the attacks won an International Emmy Award.

Forensic work by the Spanish police led them to the apartment of two suspected bombers. When officers surrounded the building, the occupants blew themselves up, also killing a Spanish policeman. Hundreds of detonators and over 20 pounds of dynamite were found in the rubble. The attacks occurred just before the Spanish elections and almost certainly affected their outcome. The Prime Minister, Jose Maria Anzar, had supported the war in Iraq despite large-scale public protests. He had already announced that he didn't intend to stand for re-election, naming Mariano Rajoy as his successor but, despite a lead in the polls, his Popular Party lost its popularity with the electors and was voted out. The incoming Prime Minister, Jose Luis Rodriguez Zapatero, withdrew Spanish troops from Iraq, bowing to overwhelming displays of anti-war feeling throughout the country.

Above: In the United States, the presidential election was hard fought between John Kerry and George W Bush.

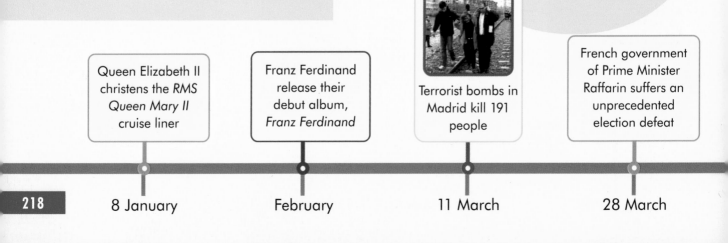

Queen Elizabeth II christens the *RMS Queen Mary II* cruise liner

Franz Ferdinand release their debut album, *Franz Ferdinand*

Terrorist bombs in Madrid kill 191 people

French government of Prime Minister Raffarin suffers an unprecedented election defeat

8 January

February

11 March

28 March

Katie Derham

Katie Derham co-presents the newly extended one hour ITV Lunchtime News with Nicholas Owen and is also co-presenter of London Tonight.

Katie, who joined ITN in January 1998, had previously been ITV News' Saturday newscaster since the beginning of 1999.

Katie was voted New TV Talent of the Year in March 1999 at the Television & Radio Industries Club (TRIC) Awards.

Katie started her journalistic career with the BBC as a researcher on Radio 4's "Moneybox". In 1995 she won the Bradford and Bingley Best Personal Finance Broadcaster Award for her work as a presenter on Radio 5 Live's "Moneycheck" programme. She also edited Radio 4's Financial World Tonight programme.

She moved across to BBC television in 1996 as a consumer affairs correspondent and subsequently became a reporter for "Film '96" and "Film "97".

Katie, has a BA(Hons) in Economics from Magdalene College, Cambridge. She is married with two daughters. She lives with her family in west London.

Above: PLO leader Yasser Arafat, who died in November 2004.

Above: DJ John Peel at the 1969 Melody Maker awards in London. He died suddenly in October 2004.

Queen Elizabeth II begins a state visit to France to celebrate the 100th anniversary of the Entente Cordiale

The abuse of Iraqi prisoners in Abu Ghraib prison is revealed on television

10 new member-states join the European Union

Part of the ceiling of Terminal 2E at Charles de Gaulle International Airport collapses, killing six people

5 April   28 April   1 May   23 May

Above: Beslan Middle School Number One, where Muslim extremists took over a thousand hostages, many of them young children.

Above: *ITV News* reporter Julian Manyon reports on the terrible events at Beslan. Despite attempts to negotiate the release of the children nearly two hundred were killed, as well as many adults.

On 1 September, children arrived at Beslan's Middle School Number One on the first day of term to celebrate the *Day of Knowledge*, as they did all across Russia. For many it was their first day at school and they came dressed in their best clothes, accompanied by their parents and bringing gifts and flowers for their new teacher. But armed Muslim extremists, angry about Russia's occupation of Chechnya, stormed the school and took over 1,000 hostages. They murdered about 20 adult male hostages, then moved the children to the school gymnasium, which was rigged with explosives. On September 3rd part of the building collapsed, apparently due to a bomb falling and exploding. Some children managed to escape but the terrorists fired on them even as they ran away. Russian Special Forces stormed the school and in the ensuing battle, 31 of the 32 terrorists were killed, along with 11 soldiers and 344 civilians – 172 of them children. As the gun fire died down, Julian Manyon and his cameraman, Sasha Lomakin, managed to get to the doorway of the gym before it was sealed off. It was Sasha who saw the terrible scene inside.

When the Boxing Day tsunami struck, ITN moved quickly to get reporters and camera teams half-way round the world to cover one of the world's worst natural disasters. *ITV News* Asia correspondent, John Irvine, was enjoying a Christmas break in the region, as were reporter Dan Rivers and some other *ITV News* staff. Bill Neely, James Mates and Mark Austin were despatched from London to join them, and they produced powerful reports of the consequences and aftermath of the tsunami.

The Darfur crisis in Sudan escalated as the Government suppressed a civil war begun by rebels wanting independence for their region in the west. Fighting between rebels and Government backed militias drove an estimated one million people from their homes – but they were just the ones in official

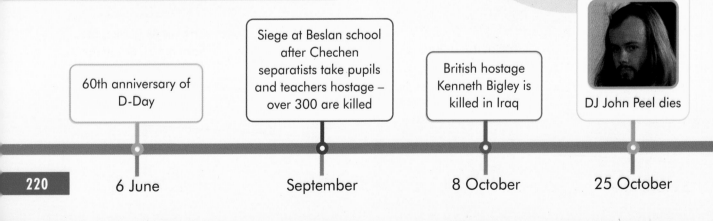

60th anniversary of D-Day

Siege at Beslan school after Chechen separatists take pupils and teachers hostage – over 300 are killed

British hostage Kenneth Bigley is killed in Iraq

DJ John Peel dies

6 June   September   8 October   25 October

TSUNAMI APPEAL
0870 60 60 900

18.18 Jan 02 IE INDIAN OCEAN   FOR MORE ON THE T

Above: Scenes of devastation, after an undersea earthquake in the Indian Ocean released a tsunami that hit the coastlines of Southern India, Indonesia, Thailand, Sri Lanka and Sumatra.

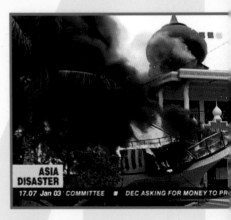

ASIA DISASTER
17.07 Jan 03 COMMITTEE ■ DEC ASKING FOR MONEY TO PR

Above: The tsunami damaged buildings, swept whole families away and wrecked entire areas. Thousands died, many of them holidaymakers enjoying some winter sun.

camps. *Channel 4 News* correspondent Jonathan Miller found rain-lashed unofficial camps where refugees had nothing to eat but leaves and their only protection against the elements was plastic sheeting.

Though the war in Iraq was officially over, US forces mounted a massive assault in November on Fallujah, the base of terrorist Abu Musab al-Zarqawi. He had links to Al Qaeda and was responsible for atrocities such as the beheading of hostage Ken Bigley. At considerable personal risk, *Channel 4 News* International Editor Lindsey Hilsum and cameraman Tim Labon produced award-winning reports on the battle for Fallujah.

Above: A refugee in one of the many poorly equipped unofficial camps during the Darfur crisis.

The animated film *The Incredibles* is released

PLO leader Yasser Arafat dies

The world's tallest bridge, the Millau over the River Tarn, is opened in France by President Jacques Chirac

An earthquake in the Indian Ocean sets off a tsunami that hits surrounding countries, killing hundreds of thousands

5 November   11 November   14 December   26 December

Above left: London News presenters, Katie Derham and Alastair Stewart.

Middle and right: The three contenders for the 2012 Olympics were London, Paris and Singapore, and Paris was the hot favourite – but at the very last minute London grabbed the prize. Princess Anne was a member of the International Olympic Commitee.

The horror of the Asian tsunami carried over in to the New Year, with the number of dead rising towards 200,000. *ITV News* produced a special programme called *Tsunami: Seven Days that Shook the World*, and Mark Austin presented the *ITV Evening News* from different locations hit by the disaster.

Pope John Paul II died on April 2nd and vast crowds flocked to Rome to pay homage to a man who had been the spiritual guide to over a billion people for 26 years. The death of the Pope meant the wedding of the Prince of Wales to Camilla Parker-Bowles was moved from April 8th to 9th. The wedding was originally planned to take place within the grounds of Windsor Castle, but it was discovered that, in order to obtain permission for this to happen, the venue would have to be made available to other couples who might wish to get married there. *ITV News* broadcast a special programme, presented by Nicholas Owen and Katie Derham, to cover the wedding. No cameras were allowed into the civil ceremony, which was finally performed across the road from Windsor Castle in the town's Guildhall. However, afterwards the couple were driven to St George's Chapel inside the castle for a blessing by the Archbishop of Canterbury, which was televised.

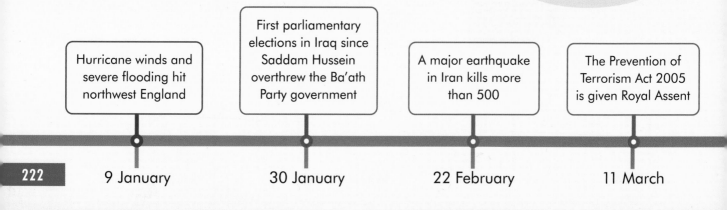

Hurricane winds and severe flooding hit northwest England

First parliamentary elections in Iraq since Saddam Hussein overthrew the Ba'ath Party government

A major earthquake in Iran kills more than 500

The Prevention of Terrorism Act 2005 is given Royal Assent

9 January

30 January

22 February

11 March

In Zimbabwe *ITV News'* Africa correspondent, Neil Connery, obtained exclusive pictures of what looked like a natural disaster – but the devastation was the policy of the country's President, Robert Mugabe, who had ordered bulldozers to flatten the homes of his political opponents.

Prime Minister Tony Blair travelled to Singapore to support Britain's bid to host the 2012 Olympic Games. Paris was hot favourite, but the vote went London's way by 54 to 50. The sober-looking London delegation literally jumped in the air when the decision was announced, during ITV's *Lunchtime News*. Presenter Alastair Stewart managed to get instant reaction to the news from Princess Anne, one of the members of the International Olympic Committee, and from Lord Coe, who led London's 2012 bid. Back in the capital, the scenes of jubilation matched those in Singapore.

The US suffered its worst natural disaster in September, when Hurricane Katrina struck the coast of Louisiana, Mississippi and Alabama. Thousands of lives were lost and homes destroyed by wind and floods. Mark Austin presented the *ITV Evening News* from the disaster zone and *ITV News'* Washington correspondent, Robert Moore, led a team of reporters to produce outstanding coverage of the desperate situation. Jon Snow presented *Channel 4 News* from New Orleans, touring the city in a boat, and assisting in rescue efforts, while *Channel 4 News* Washington correspondent, Jonathan Rugman, reported from the convention centre before it was reached by a National Guard and army convoy. President Bush was criticised for failing to mobilise the rescue effort quickly – people were left stranded, without food or clean water, while bodies floated in the flood. A super power that was so quick to help other countries in their hour of need now seemed unable to help itself.

And there were more scenes of jubilation at the Oval cricket ground when England won back the Ashes from Australia after 18 years. All the commentators agreed it was the greatest test series ever played.

Above: *ITV News* reporter Bill Neeley brought exclusive pictures of whole streets flattened in Zimbabwe, after President Mugabe sent in bulldozers to flatten opponent's homes.

Above: After Hurricane Katrina struck Louisiana, Mississippi and Alabama, Mark Austin presented the *ITV Evening News* from a flooded New Orleans, revealing the extent of the disaster.

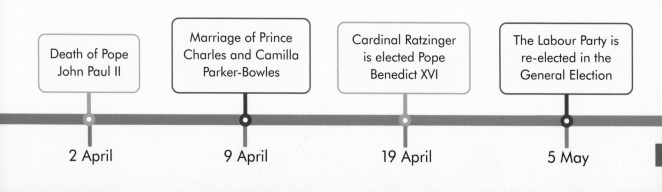

Death of Pope John Paul II

Marriage of Prince Charles and Camilla Parker-Bowles

Cardinal Ratzinger is elected Pope Benedict XVI

The Labour Party is re-elected in the General Election

2 April

9 April

19 April

5 May

BREAKING NEWS TONY BLAIR STATEMENT ON LONDON EXPLOSIONS SHORTLY

12.01 Jul 07 5 THE LATEST FROM THE ITV NEWS CHANNEL...

Top: One bomb was planted on a London bus, and went off near Russell Square.

Above: Suspected underground bombers being arrested in London.

Less than 24 hours after celebrating the news that the Olympic games were coming to London in 2012, the capital was rocked by four deadly explosions. On July 7th, four British-born suicide bombers, sympathetic to the aims of Al Qaeda, attacked three underground trains and a bus, killing 52 innocent people. ITN went on air for most of the day with open-ended coverage on *ITV News* and a special programme later in the evening. *Channel 4 News* ran news specials all through that evening.

A fortnight later the same terrible chain of events almost took place again. Four more bombers attempted similar attacks but, very fortunately, this time their bombs didn't go off. *ITV News* obtained exclusive pictures of the arrests of two of those suspected of being the bombers. A month later, *ITV News* scooped another exclusive after the shooting dead of an innocent Brazilian man, who police suspected had been involved in the second wave of attacks. *ITV News* obtained documents leaked from the Independent Police Complaints Commission inquiry into the death of Jean Charles de Menezes, which contradicted the police description of Mr Menezes' appearance and actions before they shot him.

Almost all the big stories of the year had been presented by Trevor McDonald. But, towards the end of the year, and after 32 momentous years, he stepped down from his role at ITN. Sir Trevor continues to present *Tonight* on ITV1.

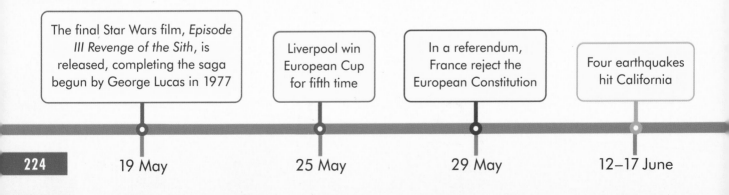

The final Star Wars film, *Episode III Revenge of the Sith*, is released, completing the saga begun by George Lucas in 1977

Liverpool win European Cup for fifth time

In a referendum, France reject the European Constitution

Four earthquakes hit California

19 May

25 May

29 May

12–17 June

Sir Trevor McDonald OBE

Trevor McDonald was a newsreader in his native Trinidad in 1962, having already worked on local newspapers and in radio. He joined the BBC World Service in London in 1969. In 1973 he joined ITN as a reporter and then became Sports correspondent in 1978. By 1980 he was Diplomatic correspondent, first on ITV, then from 1982 for *Channel 4 News*, covering many overseas conflicts. In 1989 he presented both ITV and Channel Four programmes and became a regular presenter on *News at Ten* in 1990. He was the first journalist to interview Nelson Mandela after his release from prison and also interviewed Saddam Hussein in Baghdad in 1990. In 1992 he became the sole anchor of *News at Ten*. In 1993 he interviewed President Clinton and General Colin Powell. Trevor began presenting the ITV's *Tonight* current affairs programme in 1999. When *News at Ten* ended in the same year, Trevor went on to present the *ITV Evening News* before returning to a new *News at Ten* slot in 2001 which later became the *ITV News at 10.30* in 2004. He presented the news from Kuwait city during the second Gulf War in 2003. Trevor has received more awards and honours than any other news broadcaster in Britain – among them the Richard Dimbleby Award for Outstanding Contribution to Television in 1999. He has also been voted 'most authoritative and trustworthy' newsreader by readers of *Radio Times*, and a Mori poll in 2001 named him as the most trusted television celebrity. He was knighted in 1999. He stepped down from his ITN role at the end of 2005 after more than 30 years but continues to present the *Tonight* programme for ITV1.

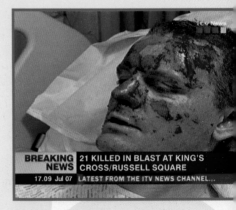

Above: Fifty six people were killed in the bomb attacks, and over seven hundred were injured.

Above: Shocked passengers call friends and relatives to see if they are safe.

Live 8 throughout the world	London is confirmed as the host for the 2012 Olympic Games, defeating favourite Paris in the final round	Four terrorist bombs on London tube and bus services kill over 50 and injure more than 700	Hurricane Katrina strikes the United States, causing widespread flooding
2 July	6 July	7 July	September

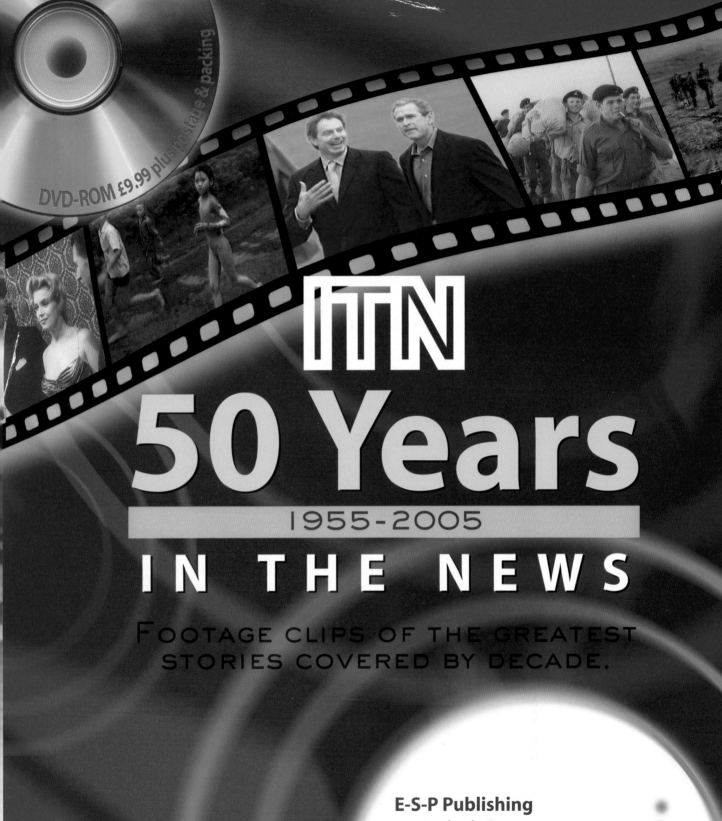

DVD-ROM £9.99 plus postage & packing

ITN

50 Years

1955-2005

IN THE NEWS

FOOTAGE CLIPS OF THE GREATEST STORIES COVERED BY DECADE.

E-S-P Publishing
17 Fenlock Court
Blenheim Office Park
Long Hanborough
Oxfordshire
OX29 8LN

Tel: 01993 882027
Email: sales@e-s-p.eu.com

E-S-P